KU-484-866

CITYSPOTS
GLASGOW

Zoë Ross

Written by Zoë Ross
Original photography by Robin Gauldie unless otherwise stated
Front cover photography courtesy of BL Images Limited/Alamy Images
Series design based on an original concept by Studio 183 Limited

Produced by Cambridge Publishing Management Limited
Project Editor: Catherine Burch
Layout: Trevor Double
Maps: PC Graphics
Reproduced by permission of Ordnance Survey on behalf of HMSO. © Crown
Copyright 2006. All rights reserved. Ordnance Survey Licence number 100035725.
Transport map: © Communicarta Ltd

Published by Thomas Cook Publishing
A division of Thomas Cook Tour Operations Limited
Company Registration No. 1450464 England
PO Box 227, Unit 18, Coningsby Road
Peterborough PE3 8SB, United Kingdom
email: books@thomascook.com
www.thomascookpublishing.com
+ 44 (0) 1733 416477
ISBN-13: 978-184157-629-9
ISBN-10: 1-84157-629-8

First edition © 2006 Thomas Cook Publishing
Text © 2006 Thomas Cook Publishing
Maps © 2006 Thomas Cook Publishing
Series Editor: Kelly Anne Pipes
Project Editor: Ross Hilton
Production/DTP: Steven Collins

Printed and bound in Spain by GraphyCems

CONTENTS

SYMBOLS & ABBREVIATIONS

The following symbols are used throughout this book:

ⓐ address   ① telephone   ⓕ fax   ⓔ email   ⓦ website address
🕐 opening times   ⊘ public transport connections   ❶ important

The following symbols are used on the maps:

𝒊	information office	○	city
✈	airport	○	large town
✚	hospital	○	small town
🛡	police station	=	motorway
🚌	bus station	—	main road
🚆	railway station	—	minor road
Ⓜ	metro	—	railway
✝	cathedral		
❶	numbers denote featured cafés & restaurants		

Hotels and restaurants are graded by approximate price as follows:
£ budget   ££ mid-range   £££ expensive

◗ *The Glasgow School of Art was designed by Charles Rennie Mackintosh*

INTRODUCING
Glasgow

Introduction

Scotland's biggest city has a high opinion of itself – and with good reason. Glasgow has a vibrant arts scene, fostering cutting-edge musicians, painters and film-makers. In recent years, it has spawned bands such as Texas, Travis, Franz Ferdinand, and Belle and Sebastian. Its nightlife is legendary, with venues that host the biggest names in rock, pop, jazz and dance music. Scottish and Celtic traditional music is celebrated in many lively pubs and bars, and the city's restaurants offer a menu that extends from the best of modern Scottish seafood and game to superb Indian, Thai, Chinese, Japanese, Tex-Mex and Asian-Pacific fusion dishes.

Glasgow has high culture too. The city is home to Scottish Opera, Scottish Royal Ballet, the BBC Scottish Symphony Orchestra, Glasgow School of Art, and some of Britain's finest museums and art galleries. It can – and does – claim to be Scotland's sporting capital, with a keenly contested rivalry between the country's two top football teams, Rangers and Celtic, as well as its international stadium at Hampden, and its pitch to host the Commonwealth Games in 2012 is a bid to put its sporting facilities on the world stage. Glasgow is also Scotland's media hub, and since the 1980s has been a centre for cutting-edge design and top-end shopping.

While it is an intensely urban place – the heart of a conurbation that sprawls across more than 650 sq km (400 sq miles) of southwest Scotland and is home to almost half the country's population – Glasgow has plenty of green spaces, with landscaped parks and city gardens laid out during the 19th century. The River Clyde winds through the heart of Glasgow on its way to the Firth of Clyde and the Atlantic, and the Scottish highlands and islands are surprisingly close to the city centre. Islands such as Bute and Arran are less than an hour away, and the wide open spaces of Loch Lomond and the Trossachs are within easy reach.

And although the psychological gulf between bold, brash Glasgow and well-bred, genteel Edinburgh sometimes seems unbridgeable, Edinburgh is in fact fewer than 40 minutes away by rail, so its attractions are also easily accessible, even on a short break.

⬤ *George Square is dominated by the grand City Chambers*

When to go

SEASONS & CLIMATE

Scottish weather is noticeably colder than southern England's, but Glasgow's climate is mellowed by the Atlantic, and temperatures rarely fall to freezing point, even in mid-winter, and only rarely rise as high as 25°C (77°F) in mid-summer. However, that same Atlantic influence means that overcast skies and rain are not unlikely at any time of year, so come prepared. If you plan to venture beyond the city into the hills and moors of Argyll or to walk a stretch of the West Highland Way, good boots and waterproof outerwear are essential.

Glasgow has plenty of indoor attractions for a winter visit, but it is undeniably more attractive in spring (April–May) when early blooming daffodils, tulips and crocuses bring a blaze of colour to its parks and gardens, and in summer when Scotland's long, light evenings allow plenty of time for exploring. September and October, as leaves turn autumnal and early frosts can bring crisp, clear days, can be perfect times for trips out of town.

COSTS

The cost of a visit to Glasgow is broadly in line with costs in the rest of the UK. That said, the cost of a hotel room, a night out or a restaurant meal is somewhat less than in London. Taxis and public transport are significantly cheaper than they are in London.

ANNUAL EVENTS

Glasgow has a huge year-round programme of arts and music festivals and exhibitions.

January

Hogmanay. New Year's Eve is raucously celebrated all over Scotland, and Glasgow's Hogmanay is no exception. It kicks off in George Square at 21.00 on 31 December and carries on until well into the early hours of 1 January, featuring live rock, traditional music and family entertainment. Tickets cost £2.50. ❶ 0871 200 3940

For three weeks each January, the city hosts the **Celtic Connections festival**. An array of big names from Ireland, Wales and Brittany, and musicians in the Celtic tradition from as far away as Canada, the USA and Australia descend on the city with their fiddles and pipes. Ⓦ www.celticconnections.com

🔺 *The River Clyde runs through the very urban city of Glasgow*

Burns Night (25 January), the birthday of Scotland's National Poet is celebrated with whisky, haggis, pipe music and poetry.

February
Glasgow Film Festival has become a showcase for work by leading Scottish and international film directors.
ⓦ www.glasgowfilmfestival.org.uk

A Play, a Pie and a Pint, in pubs and theatres at lunchtime across town from February to May, showcases new and lively work by top Scottish playwrights and performers.

March
Given the Irish roots of so many Glaswegians, it's not surprising that **St Patrick's Day** (17 March) is a popular celebration in many pubs. What is more surprising is that St Andrew's Day (30 November), the day of Scotland's patron saint, slips by almost unnoticed.

The Miller Glasgow International Comedy Festival features top stand-up comics (see page 12).

April
Glasgow International Festival of Contemporary Visual Art showcases adventurous and challenging commissioned work and installations. At the **Glasgow Art Fair** more than 50 galleries show the works of selected artists.

June–August
These are lively festival months with events including the **West End Festival** and its **Midsummer Carnival parade**, international performers at the **Glasgow International Jazz Festival**, a month of open-air drama at the **Bard in the Botanics Summer Shakespeare**

Festival, and the tartan pageantry of the **Glasgow International Piping Festival** (ⓦ www.pipingfestival.co.uk).

September
The Merchant City Festival is a feast of music, drama and visual arts, while in George Square **Whisky Live** (ⓦ www.whiskylive.com) is part of a European-wide whisky-tasting event.

October
Big Big World is a celebration of world music, with artists from Africa, Asia and South America. ⓦ www.soundsfine.co.uk

November
Glasgay! is Britain's largest gay arts festival, with film, theatre, comedy and music. ⓦ www.glasgay.co.uk

NATIONAL PUBLIC HOLIDAYS
Public holidays are similar to those in England but do not include Easter Monday. Instead, Scots take two days off to recover from Hogmanay. Traditionally, many shops and businesses close down for the Glasgow Fair, a holiday fortnight in early August, but this has virtually died out and most of Glasgow is open for business throughout August.

New Year Bank Holidays 1 & 2 January
Good Friday April/May
May Bank Holiday 1st Monday
August Bank Holiday 1st Monday
Christmas Day 25 December
Boxing Day 26 December

Comedy festival

Every March, for just over two weeks, Glasgow splits its sides as it becomes embroiled in the annual Comedy Festival. Inspired by the success of the comedy aspect of Edinburgh's summer arts festival, the Miller Glasgow International Comedy Festival (Ⓦ www. glasgowcomedyfestival.com) began in 2002 and has proved a sure-fire hit, expanding annually and bringing some much-needed lightheartedness at the end of another winter.

Venues all over the city are utilised for the event, from the smallest pub theatre to the renowned Stand Comedy Club (see page 32), to large-scale auditoriums such as the Theatre Royal. Even going out for a quiet drink is likely to prove difficult, as many of the city centre bars get in on the act. The reputation of the festival has grown in a remarkably short space of time, so much so that big-name British comedians, such as Paul Merton, Ronnie Corbett and Jimmy Carr, are keen to sign up to the programme. International names, such as Joan Rivers, also descend on the city to enlighten audiences (which number around 40,000 people) with their own brand of humour.

In total, there are some 270 shows staged in more than 30 venues throughout the fortnight. Some events are also geared exclusively towards children, while comedy drama is staged at venues such as the Citizens Theatre. Additionally, there are some improvisational comedy events and comic films (at Glasgow Film Theatre), which all form part of this laughter-fest.

Tickets sell out fast, particularly for the big-name shows, but can be obtained online or by phoning Ⓦ 0141 552 2070.

▶ *A great night out at The Stand Comedy Club*

History

The site where Glasgow city centre now stands was settled as early as AD 550 by monks from Ireland, led by St Mungo. Glasgow's first cathedral, named after St Mungo, was consecrated in the 12th century AD. The city's university was founded in 1451.

Handily located between the Highland and Lowland regions, Glasgow became a prosperous medieval trade centre and port – and it was less vulnerable than Edinburgh, the country's capital, to English invasion.

But it was the union of Scotland with England in 1707 that made the city its first fortune, importing tobacco, sugar and rum from English colonies in America and the Caribbean that had been opened to Scottish trade for the first time. Some of the most impressive buildings of Glasgow's Merchant City district date from those 18th-century boom years.

The Atlantic trade was damaged by the secession of Britain's American colonies in 1776, but Glasgow's entrepreneurs branched out into other industries. The city was perfectly placed to take advantage of the new technologies of the Industrial Revolution, with coalfields and iron ore on its doorstep and the River Clyde as its gateway to world markets. In the 19th century it became one of the powerhouses of British industry and the greatest ship-building city in the world – the words 'Clyde built' became synonymous with sturdy reliability.

Glasgow also had two handy sources of labour close by. In the 1840s the Scottish Highlands and Ireland were struck by famine, and hundreds of thousands of people were drawn to the city in search of work. Glasgow's urban slums became a byword for social deprivation, while its industrial workers became a vanguard of the labour movement. Meanwhile, many of its wealthy capitalists endowed the city with grandiose public buildings, museums and concert halls, and the city became a noted centre for the arts and sciences.

World War I, the decline of the British Empire and the Depression of the 1930s all hit Glasgow hard, and German air raids on the shipyards of the Clyde caused much damage and loss of life during World War II. Postwar Glasgow sank into decline as the heavy industries on which its economy was based collapsed, and the search for new sources of employment and prosperity seemed fruitless. Well-meant efforts to re-house the city's workers in the 1950s and 1960s often backfired, with new housing estates such as Easterhouse displaying many of the same intractable social problems as the city's slums. Drug and alcohol abuse and violent crime remain an issue in Glasgow's deprived suburbs even today.

With the 1980s, however, came an upturn in Glasgow's fortunes as new technologies and service industries made an impact on unemployment, and the city began to re-invent itself as a cultural capital and tourism destination and centre of educational excellence. In the early years of the 21st century, Glasgow has rebuilt its reputation as one of Europe's most vibrant and youthful cities.

Lifestyle

Glasgow prides itself on its friendliness – and Glaswegians love to draw mischievous comparisons with Edinburgh and the capital's reputation for dour reserve. It's certainly easier to fall into conversation with Glaswegians than with the natives of virtually any other British city. Football is of course a favourite topic, and any male expressing a lack of interest in the beautiful game will be regarded with sympathetic disbelief. But before expressing support for one or other of Glasgow's 'Old Firm' teams, be aware that football loyalties are deep and passions run high.

The traditional Glasgow lifestyle, with its high consumption of alcohol, tobacco, fried food, sugar and salt, is notoriously the least healthy in Europe. In some of the city's poorest areas, male life expectancy is under 60 years, with heart disease and cancer the main killers. But a wider choice of diet and campaigns against alcohol abuse and smoking are gradually easing young Glaswegians towards a healthier lifestyle than that of their parents – not least because many younger people recognise that smoking and sporting fitness are incompatible.

Glaswegians love dressing up and going out – especially at weekends. That said, bars, clubs and pubs are lively almost any night of the week. These days, classy style bars almost outnumber old-style pubs in the city centre. Glaswegians are also among the world's most enthusiastic movie-goers. Sport – which in Glasgow means football – is an obsession. For most Glaswegian males Saturday afternoon is sacrosanct to the game, and it's virtually impossible to find a bar or pub without a TV screen tuned to the day's big fixture.

With a climate that can turn cold and wet at any time, Glasgow's lifestyle is an indoor one for much of the year. Ironically, the smoking edict has created an instant outdoor drinking culture, with many pubs and bars offering outdoor tables – sheltered by umbrellas and warmed by gas heaters – to evade the ban on smoking indoors.

There's also a long and healthier tradition of getting out of the city on summer weekends to take a ferry 'doon the watter' to the islands of the Firth of Clyde, spend a day on the beaches of Ayrshire, walk in the hills of Argyll or the Pentlands, or sail on Loch Lomond.

▲ Glasgow has no shortage of fashionable cafés and bars when you need a break

Culture

Glasgow emerged from the cultural shadow of Edinburgh in 1990, when against the odds it won the European City of Culture title, ushering in an exciting new era for the arts. But in truth the city already had a strong cultural background that spanned high art – in the shape of ballet, opera, classical music, painting and sculpture – as well as the low humour of music halls and comedy theatres. Both still flourish.

Performance arts

Edinburgh may be the Scottish capital, but it is Glasgow that is home to most of the national performing companies. In terms of classical music the BBC Scottish Symphony Orchestra (which performs at Glasgow City Halls) and Scottish Opera (which performs classics such as *Don Giovanni*, as well as selections from a range of operas in its annual Opera in the City concerts) are both based here.

In terms of theatre, too, Glasgow takes the lead. The Theatre Royal and the King's Theatre both stage touring West End productions, usually large-scale musicals. The Tron is home to more avant-garde productions, as well as contemporary dance, jazz concerts and comedy acts. The Citizens Theatre is the city's repertory theatre, staging new works by both Scottish and international playwrights.

One of the newest ventures in Scotland is the National Theatre of Scotland, which performs all round the country; in Glasgow it makes its home in an incongruous tower block along the M8, which makes a great spot for experimental performances.

Scottish Ballet, also based in Glasgow, has had a great resurgence of late, performing newly commissioned pieces.

BBC Scottish Symphony Orchestra ⊚ City Halls, Candleriggs ① 0141 552 0909 ⓦ www.bbc.co.uk/bbcssco

Scottish Opera ⊚ Theatre Royal, 282 Hope Street ① 0141 248 4567 ⓦ www.scottishopera.org.uk

Theatre Royal ⊚ 282 Hope Street ① 0141 240 1133 ⓦ www.theatreroyalglasgow.com

King's Theatre ⊚ 297 Bath Street ① 0141 240 1111 ⓦ www.kings-glasgow.co.uk

The Tron ⊚ 63 Trongate ① 0141 552 4267 ⓦ www.tron.co.uk

Citizens Theatre ⊚ 119 Gorbals Street ① 0141 429 0022 ⓦ www.citz.co.uk

National Theatre of Scotland ⊚ 25 Soutra Place, Cranhill ① 0141 781 2034 ⓦ www.nationaltheatrescotland.com

Scottish Ballet ⊚ 261 West Princes Street ① 0141 331 2931 ⓦ www.scottishballet.co.uk

▲ *The BBC Scottish Symphony Orchestra*

Visual arts

Many of Glasgow's 19th-century plutocrats became patrons of the arts, endowing the city with world-class art galleries and museums such as Kelvingrove (see page 85) and the amazingly eclectic Burrell Collection, with its accumulated treasures from all over the world (see page 98).

The most famous artist and designer associated with Glasgow is, of course, Charles Rennie Mackintosh and there is a one-day ticket that covers the 'Mackintosh Trail' taking in sights such as the Willow Tea Rooms (see page 77) and the Scotland Street School Museum (see page 100) to fully appreciate the artist's great vision (❶ 0141 946 6600 Ⓦ www.seeglasgow.com).

Glasgow School of Art (see page 70), also designed by Charles Rennie Mackintosh in 1896, has fostered a huge number of talented artists. Work by cutting-edge artists is on show at the annual Glasgow Art Fair (see page 10), held each year in April on George Square and at the prestigious Glasgow International Exhibition in May.

MUSEUMS

Glasgow was born out of the Industrial Revolution and many of its museums are keen to preserve this history, including the Scotland Street School Museum (see page 100), the Glasgow Police Museum (see page 70) and, most importantly, the Clydebuilt Scottish Maritime Museum, examining how important the river was to the success of the city.

▶ *Twenty-first century Glasgow*

Shopping

If you're a shopaholic you'll love Glasgow, particularly if you're after designer names and high-end high street gear. There's the fair share of typical Scottish goods such as tartan, cashmere or whisky, but Glasgow is far more focused on style than souvenirs.

OPENING HOURS AND TAX

Standard opening hours are 09.00–18.00 Mon–Sat, although larger stores usually stay open until later on Thursdays and also open on Sundays with shorter opening hours.

❶ Value added tax is included in the price of most purchases. Non-EU citizens can claim this back on leaving the UK if they obtain a form when buying and hand it in at customs at the airport.

WHERE TO SHOP

The main shopping area in the city centre is the pedestrianised triangle that is Sauchiehall Street, Argyle Street and, most importantly, Buchanan Street. Here you'll find many indoor shopping areas as well as high-street fashion outlets like Karen Millen and Hobbs, and department stores.

The Merchant City area and the West End, particularly Byres Road, are the primary central areas for second-hand goods such as clothes and books as well as antiques at places such as De Courcy's Antique Craft Arcade. Antiques are also a major feature at the Scottish Exhibition and Conference Centre (Junction 19, M8 ⓦ www.antiquesshowscotland.com).

▶ *The elegant atrium of the shopping centre at Princes Square*

MALLS

Glasgow abounds with indoor shopping areas – no bad thing given the high chance of rain at any given time of day or year. The best-known and most elegant shopping mall in the city is Princes Square (see page 76) on Buchanan Street, where quality names such as Jo Malone and Space NK sell their wares over a four-floor emporium with stylish cafés on the basement level.

● *If you like markets you'll love The Barras*

Buchanan Galleries is less sumptuous but larger, and is home to stores such as Habitat and John Lewis. The 19th-century Argyll Arcade is reminiscent of London's elegant Victorian arcades and is lined with more than 30 jewellers. The vast St Enoch Shopping Centre (see page 76) is more family orientated and concentrates on high street chains such as bhs. Meanwhile, Victorian Village has its focus strongly in the past, and is a great place for vintage clothing and costume jewellery.

Merchant Square in Merchant City (see page 75) is the ideal place for gifts, while The Italian Centre (see page 74) brings the best of Italian design to Glasgow in both household goods and clothing, including branches of Armani and Versace.

MARKETS

One of the most famous markets in the country is The Barras, an antique-cum-flea market just to the east of the city centre (see page 72). If it's a nice day, prepare to spend at least a couple of hours here browsing the stalls and jostling with locals and the vociferous market traders.

LOCAL CRAFTS

There are numerous places in Glasgow where you can find traditional cashmere, tartan, Celtic jewellery, whisky and other typically Scottish goods. But for something that is more specific to the city, why not buy some Charles Rennie Mackintosh inspired pieces, such as mugs and tea towels, from the Willow Tearooms gift shop (see page 77)? Nothing says 'Glasgow' quite so much as these Arts and Crafts designs.

Eating & drinking

Scotland may still have a reputation for serving everything fried, but in recent years the city has earned the tag as the best place to eat in Britain outside London. There is a vast array of top-class restaurants, fashionable cafés and bars all over the city, as well as a wide range of budget options. Pub culture is, of course, alive and well, and there are plenty of traditional options. Unlike Edinburgh, though, Glasgow has embraced modernity with vigour and if you're after trendy décor while you drink, this is the city for you.

Scottish restaurants focus heavily on meat and fish, although vegetarians should always be able to find a suitable option on most menus. Mono, near the St Enoch Centre (see page 76), is an elegant vegetarian restaurant with occasional live music.

There's no hard or fast rule as to whether restaurants include service charges on their bill or not – some do and some don't. So check your bill when paying. If service is not included, it's customary to leave a tip of 10–15 per cent of the cost of the meal. Tips aren't required in pubs if you're only drinking, even though some bars have the annoying habit of returning your change in a saucer in the expectation of a little gratuity.

RESTAURANT CATEGORIES

The following price guide used throughout the book indicates the average price per head for a 2–3 course à la carte dinner, excluding drinks. Lunch will usually be a little cheaper in each category and many restaurants also offer fixed-price menus.

£ = up to £20   ££ = £20–£30   £££ = above £30

Lunch is usually served between midday and 14.30, and dinner between 18.00 and 23.30, but many restaurants stay open all day with a continuous service.

ⓘ Since 26 March 2006 all public places, including restaurants, pubs and bars, have become strictly non-smoking.

ETHNIC RESTAURANTS

Glasgow has the best reputation for Indian food in Scotland, so if you're a curry fan you'll be spoilt for choice here. Asian restaurants can be found all over the city, but some of the best are located in the West End district.

Italians began to emigrate to Glasgow in the 1850s and the first half of the 20th century, and today the city has the third-largest Italian community in Britain. Inevitably, many of the immigrants turned to catering to earn their living, and Glasgow boasts a long tradition of Italian food, from elegant restaurants to family-run trattorias to Italian delis and cafés.

These two regions may dominate, but all manner of ethnic food can be found in the city, from Greek to Mexican to Thai to Japanese.

MARKETS & PICNICS

The Glasgow Farmers' Market at Mansfield Park (ⓐ Hyndland Street) is the city's best food market, selling fruit, vegetables, game, seafood and Scottish cheeses. It is held twice a month on the second and fourth Saturdays. There are plenty of tempting samples on offer, and traditional Scottish music to add to the atmosphere. There are also numerous delis in the city, including the well-known Fratelli Sarti, which sells Italian delicacies.

SPECIALITIES

Meat plays an important part in Scottish cuisine and you'll see plenty of Aberdeen Angus beef, venison and lamb on restaurant menus, and game such as pheasant and partridge in season. Cullen Skink is a delicious haddock and potato soup that is very heartening on a cold winter's day, while Arbroath Smokies are smoked haddock that originate from the eastern coastal town. And, of course, fish and chips (known as 'fish supper' in Scotland) of high quality are available all over the city.

For a savoury snack many bakers sell Bridies, which are a take on the Cornish pasty but made with puff pastry instead of shortcrust. Another savoury snack are oatcakes, delicious when served with Scottish cheeses. For a sweet tea-time snack you can't go wrong with traditional Scottish shortbread. Ice cream, too, has a long-standing tradition in Glasgow, given its large Italian community.

Whisky, both malt and blended, is the most famous Scottish drink, made in distilleries around the country, but Glasgow also boasts two distilleries of its own. Tours of Whyte & Mackay

HAGGIS

Haggis is probably the most famous Scottish dish, although its description may not appeal to all tastes. Similar to a ball-shaped sausage, it consists of sheep's intestines, heart and liver, minced with onion, oatmeal and various spices contained within the animal's stomach lining, then boiled and traditionally served with mashed swede and potato (neeps and tatties). If the real thing doesn't appeal, vegetarian haggis made with pulses, vegetables and nuts is increasingly available, although most Scots find the notion an aberration.

(💿 310 St Vincent Street ☎ 0141 248 5771) and the Speyside Distillery
(💿 Duchess Road, Rutherglen ☎ 0141 647 4464
🌐 www.speysidedistillery.co.uk) can be arranged. Glasgow also
has its own brewery, Tennents Caledonian, right in the centre of the
city (Wellpark Brewery 💿 161 Duke Street), which brews the famous
Tennents lager.

🔺 *Weather permitting, you can enjoy a leisurely meal outside at Piazza Italia*

Entertainment & nightlife

Glasgow is the hub of entertainment and nightlife in Scotland. As well as theatre and classical music, many of its live music, comedy stores and nightclubs have legendary status and keep the city buzzing year round. Whether you want to tap your feet to traditional Scottish music or dance until the early hours beneath flashing disco lights, you'll never be short of evening entertainment in the city.

LISTINGS & WHAT'S ON
❶ Glasgow's main listings magazine (which also covers Edinburgh) is the weekly *The List*, available from the tourist office and most newsagents. As well as articles about events relevant to both cities, it gives full listings of club nights, cinemas, theatre, gay events and comedy. It also has an online source at ⓦ www.list.co.uk

CINEMA

Glaswegians are avid cinema-goers, hence the roaring success of the annual Glasgow Film Festival, and the city boasts plenty of chain movie houses. However, there are also specialist cinemas. The Glasgow Film Theatre is considered the finest cinema in Scotland and is the setting for independent films from around the world, as well as arthouse movies. It's also host to the annual Renault French Film Festival, celebrating new offerings from across the Channel. As part of the Science Centre the GSC IMAX cinema screens 3-D movies in digital sound. In addition, the city itself has contributed to the world of film as the birthplace of numerous international film stars, including Deborah Kerr, Robert Carlyle, John Hannah and David McCallum.

Glasgow Film Theatre ⓐ 12 Rose Street ⓣ 0141 332 8128
ⓦ www.gft.org.uk
GSC IMAX Theatre ⓐ Glasgow Science Centre, Pacific Quay
ⓣ 0141 420 5000 ⓦ www.gsc.org.uk

COMEDY

As birthplace to one of Britain's most popular and successful
comedians, Billy Connolly, it's not surprising that humour is a strong
fixture on the Glasgow entertainment scene. There are dozens of
regular venues and open-mic nights where budding comedians can
try their hand with the inevitable hecklers, while stand-up comedy
with professional comedians has been boosted even further by the
Miller Glasgow Comedy Festival (see page 12). The Stand Comedy Club
is an offshoot from its extremely popular branch in Edinburgh and is
the most successful comedy venue in the city. There's also the chain
Jongleurs, which features both home-grown talents and touring well-
known names. The music scene is equally live and kicking.

The Stand Comedy Club ⓐ 333 Woodlands Road ⓣ 0870 600 6055
ⓦ www.thestand.co.uk
Blackfriars ⓐ 36 Bell Street ⓣ 0141 552 5924 ⓛ Fri & Sat
Curlers ⓐ 260 Byres Road ⓣ 0141 338 6511 ⓛ Fri & Sat
Jongleurs ⓐ Renfrew Street ⓣ 0870 787 0707 ⓦ www.jongleurs.com

LIVE MUSIC

Glasgow has given birth to innumerable bands that first gigged in
their native city and went on to become international names. New
talents regularly emerge from live music venues such as the
legendary King Tut's Wah Wah Hut – where Oasis broke into the big
time and where the emphasis is on indie music with a nod to rock,

funk, punk and fusion. At the other end of the musical scale, acoustic folk is celebrated with regular sessions at venues such as The Star Folk Club, while the Grand Ole Opry emulates Nashville's icon of country & western music by staging concerts by both home-grown and American country stars. Big name stadium rock, featuring bands such as The Rolling Stones and Bon Jovi, is held at Hampden Park football stadium.

Grand Ole Opry ⓐ 2/4 Govan Road ⓣ 0141 429 5396
King Tut's Wah Wah Hut ⓐ 272a St Vincent Street ⓣ 0141 221 5279
The Star Folk Club ⓐ St Andrew's Square ⓣ 0141 563 0454
ⓦ www.starfolkclub.com

CLUBBING

Glasgow is Scotland's clubbing capital and a range of clubs all over the city cater to all manner of tastes – from house to electronica to trance. Some of the most popular are listed below. Glasgow's gay district can be found in the Merchant City quarter, where clubs such as The Coco Club and the long-established Bennet's are located.

The Arches ⓐ 253 Argyle Street ⓣ 0141 565 1035
Bamboo ⓐ 51 West Regent Street ⓣ 0141 332 1067
Bennet's ⓐ 90 Glassford Street ⓣ 0141 552 5761
Chinawhite ⓐ 158–166 Bath Street ⓣ 0141 331 4068
Club Buddha ⓐ 142 St Vincent Street ⓣ 0141 243 2212
Destiny ⓐ Cambridge Street ⓣ 0141 353 6555
Garage ⓐ 490 Sauchiehall Street ⓣ 0141 332 1120
The Coco Club ⓐ 18 Jamaica Street ⓣ 0141 847 0820

◗ *Dramatic happenings at the Celtic Connections festival*

Sport & relaxation

SPECTATOR SPORTS
Football

Football is almost a religion in Glasgow, but locals are only one of two things – a Celtic fan or a Rangers fan. Celtic (in green and white) play at their home ground of Celtic Park and tickets to matches can be obtained either online at Ⓦ www.celticfc.net or from the ticket office on ❶ 0870 060 1888. Rangers' (in blue and white strip) home ground is the Ibrox Stadium and tickets there can be obtained by calling ❶ 0870 600 1993. Tickets, however, sell out very fast.

Ice hockey

Having reached Scotland from Canada, ice hockey is now a popular spectator sport in Glasgow. The local team are the Paisley Pirates.
Lagoon Leisure ❸ Centre Mill Street ❶ 0141 889 7373

Rugby

The city's main rugby team is the Glasgow Warriors who play at their home ground of Firhill. Tickets can be purchased on ❶ 0131 346 5100.

> ### OLD FIRM RIVALRIES
> Rivalries between football teams are common in all sporting nations, but the contest between Rangers and Celtic, known as the 'Old Firm', is fiercely heartfelt. In part this is due to religious sectarianism that remains strong throughout Glasgow – Celtic are a Catholic team, Rangers are Protestant. In recent years both teams have made efforts to remove the sectarian aspect from their game.

PARTICIPATION SPORTS

Canoeing

Head out to Loch Lomond where the company Can You Experience? organises both guided and unguided canoe trips and hire. What better way to take in the breathtaking scenery of Britain's largest inland waterway? ⓐ Loch Lomond Shores, Balloch ⓣ 01389 602576 ⓦ www.canyouexperience.com

Climbing

On Glasgow's Southside the Glasgow Climbing Centre offers indoor 'rock' climbing within this converted church. Instruction is available for beginners, and if you then want to do the real thing in the great outdoors staff will give advice on the best places to go.
ⓐ Ibrox Church, 534 Paisley Road West ⓣ 0141 427 9550
ⓦ www.glasgowclimbingcentre.co.uk ⓛ noon–22.00 Mon–Fri, 09.00–18.00 Sat, 10.00–19.00 Sun. Admission charge

Golf

There are more than 40 golf courses on the outskirts of Glasgow, including the World of Golf Centre in the Clydebank area, which offers tuition, floodlit ranges and a putting green.
ⓐ 2700 Great Western Road ⓣ 0141 944 4141 ⓛ 09.00–22.00 Mon–Fri, 08.00–22.00 Sat & Sun

Skiing

On Glasgow's Southside there is a floodlit ski slope that is suitable for both beginners (instructors are available) and experienced skiers.
ⓐ Glasgow Ski and Snowboard Centre Bellahouston Park, 16 Drumbreck Road ⓣ 0141 427 4991 ⓛ 10.00–22.00 Mon–Fri, 10.00–21.00 Sat. Admission charge

Accommodation

Glasgow has accommodation to suit all budgets, from luxurious hotels to basic lodgings and motels, to quaint B&Bs both in and outside the city. Some hotels include breakfast in the room rate and some don't, so check before you book. In the larger hotels breakfast is likely to be a full Scottish affair, including black pudding and haggis.

Out of season it's not always necessary to book in advance, but this is a conference city so it's wise to check whether any major event is taking place at the time of your stay. Finding hotels on the web or from the tourist office is also straightforward (ⓦ www.visitscotland.com).

HOTELS & GUEST HOUSES

Babbity Bowster £ More famous for its downstairs bar (see page 77), the upstairs rooms in this 18th-century building are excellent value for money even if they're slightly lacking in amenities.
ⓐ 16–18 Blackfriars Street ⓣ 0141 552 5055

Bewley's Hotel £ A bargain price with a stylish touch. Standard double rooms, family rooms and two penthouse suites (for a little

PRICE RATING
The following ratings indicate the average price per double room per night. Some rooms may be more or less expensive than the rating suggests, depending on high or low season.

£ = up to £60   **££** = £60–£150   **£££** = above £150

extra) are all available in this pleasant hotel right in the heart of the city centre. ❸ 110 Bath Street ❶ 0141 353 0800
ⓦ www.bewleyshotels.com

Express by Holiday Inn £ No mod-cons at all here – just a bed and bathroom. But its central location makes it ideal for sightseeing and bar-crawling. ❸ Stockwell Street & Clyde Street ❶ 0141 548 5000
ⓦ www.hieglasgow.co.uk

Rennie Mackintosh City Hotel £ Set in a restored Victorian townhouse, the décor here has been inspired by the ubiquitous designs of Charles Rennie Mackintosh (see page 74), making for a true Glaswegian atmosphere. It also has the benefit of a garden – a rare thing in such a central location. The generous Scottish breakfast is included in the price. ❸ 218 Renfrew Street ❶ 0141 333 9992

● *The stylish Rennie Mackintosh City Hotel*

Arthouse Hotel ££ Contemporary art plays a big role here, especially as students from Glasgow School of Art are allowed to display their work here. The rooms are equally up-to-date in their design, and the Arthouse Grill is an attraction for residents and non-guests.
ⓐ 129 Bath Street ⓣ 0141 221 6789 ⓦ www.arthousehotel.com

Brunswick Hotel ££ In the heart of Merchant City, this minimalist boutique hotel is an ideal base if you're planning a night on the tiles. ⓐ 104–108 Brunswick Street ⓣ 0141 552 0001
ⓦ www.brunswickhotel.co.uk

Kirklee Hotel ££ If Glasgow's bustle gets too much for you, Kirklee is the perfect antidote – in-room breakfast, a friendly lounge and a rose garden belie the central position of this boutique hotel.
ⓐ 11 Kensington Gate ⓣ 0141 334 5555 ⓦ www.kirkleehotel.co.uk

Malmaison ££ Set in a converted church, Malmaison is a chain hotel that does away with the concept of chain hotels. It's stylish and personable, with elegant rooms decorated in bold colours and a champagne bar in the basement. ⓐ 278 West George Street
ⓣ 0141 572 1000 ⓦ www.malmaison.com

Radisson SAS Hotel ££ You won't feel pampered or special here, but if you want all the mod-cons of a large chain hotel, as well as an indoor pool and spa facilities right in the centre of the city, you can't go wrong with the Radisson. ⓐ 301 Argylle Street ⓣ 0141 204 3333
ⓦ www.radissonsas.com

ABode Glasgow £££ Choose your room type by its title – Comfortable (at the cheaper end) to Fabulous (at top-price end), and

Desirable and Enviable in between. All types have DVD players and wide-screen TVs. ⓐ 129 Bath Street ⓣ 0141 221 6789 ⓦ www.abodehotels.co.uk

City Inn £££ A lovely place to take in the river views and ponder on the area's great shipbuilding history. The onsite restaurant is also highly rated. ⓐ Finnieston Quay ⓣ 0141 240 1002 ⓦ www.cityinn.com

Langs £££ If it's raining outside and you don't feel like sightseeing, you can always stay in your room and play with the PlayStation provided. The rooms themselves are all that one expects from luxury modern hotels – dark wood, crisp linen and contemporary art. There's also a spa and an onsite Pan-Asian restaurant. ⓐ 2 Port Dundas Place ⓣ 0141 333 1500 ⓦ www.langshotels.co.uk

One Devonshire Gardens £££ This award-winning hotel provides the bed of choice for visiting celebrities and other wealthy guests, with its beautifully designed rooms all complete with wide-screen TVs. Despite this nod to modernity, however, the hotel's charm lies in its Victorian details including stained-glass windows. ⓐ 1 Devonshire Gardens ⓣ 0141 339 2001 ⓦ www.onedevonshiregardens.com

SELF-CATERING

For general information about Glasgow rental apartments see ⓦ www.glasgowhotelsandapartments.co.uk

Number 52 Charlotte Street ££ If you can't afford to live in a Georgian townhouse designed by Robert Adam, you can at least stay in one for a few days by renting one of these six serviced

apartments. A cleaner comes daily to tidy and change linen, but breakfast is not included. ❸ 52 Charlotte Street ❶ 0845 230 5252 ⓦ www.52charlottestreet.co.uk

The Spires ££ Wonderfully elegant central apartments, some of which have a terrace. ❸ The Pinnacle, 1/10, 160 Bothwell Street ❶ 0845 270 0090 ⓦ www.thespires.co.uk

Somerset Merchant City £££ A central aparthotel – which means rooms with a kitchen and a general cleaner but no other facilities. Great for families or those who want a little more independence than a hotel offers. ❸ 1–19 Albion Street ❶ 0141 553 4288 ⓦ www.the-ascott.com

⬥ Langs Hotel offers luxury in a modern setting

YOUTH HOSTELS

Euro Hostel Glasgow £ There's a choice of single, double or dormitory accommodation here, with the added benefit that breakfast is included, but there's also a kitchen if you want to do your own thing. ⓐ 318 Clyde Street ⓣ 0141 222 2828 ⓦ www.euro-hostels.co.uk

SY Hostel £ You need to be a member of the Youth Hostel Association to stay here, in dormitory rooms that sleep between four and six people. A good West End location. ⓐ 8 Park Terrace ⓣ 0141 332 3004 ⓦ www.syha.org.uk

CAMPING

The countryside around Glasgow, especially Loch Lomond, makes for wonderful camping holidays in summer and all campsites are within easy reach of the city. Here's a selection:

Cashel Camping & Caravan Park Balmaha ⓐ Rowardennan, Glasgow ⓣ 01360 870234

Clyde Valley Caravan Park ⓐ Kirkfieldbank, Lanark ⓣ 01555 663951

Cobleand Campsite & Caravan Park ⓐ Aberfoyle Forest, Cobleland ⓦ www.forestholidays.co.uk

Craigendmuir ⓐ Park Stepps, Glasgow ⓣ 0141 779 2973 ⓦ www.craigendmuir.co.uk

Gart Caravan Park ⓐ Stirling Road, Callander ⓣ 01877 330002

Inverbeg Holiday Park ⓐ Inverbeg, Luss ⓣ 01436 860267

Loch Lomond Holiday Park ⓐ Loch Lomond, Inveruglas, Argyll ⓣ 01301 704224 ⓦ www.lochlomond-lodges.co.uk

Lomond Woods Holiday Park ⓐ Balloch ⓣ 01389 759475

Tullichewan Holiday Park ⓐ Old Luss Road, Balloch, Alexandria ⓣ 01389 759475

THE BEST OF GLASGOW

Glasgow is a large, sprawling city and if you only have a short time to visit its main sights it's probably best to take one of the hop-on hop-off buses that stop at major locations around the city.

TOP 10 ATTRACTIONS

- **Kelvingrove Art Gallery & Museum** Glasgow's finest art collection includes works by Rembrandt and Constable, while the museum features a wonderful natural history section (see page 85).

- **Burrell Collection** More than 9,000 works of art from all over the world (see page 98).

- **Charles Rennie Mackintosh** The master architect and designer left the most distinctive mark on the city in places such as the Willow Tearooms (see page 77).

- **The Barras** One of the most famous markets in Britain (see page 72).

- **Glasgow Cathedral** This medieval edifice dominates the cityscape (see page 64).

- **Pollok House** A wonderfully preserved Georgian house set within its own country park (see page 94).

- **Gallery of Modern Art** The finest collection of modern art in the city (see page 68).

- **Glasgow Science Centre** Built for the Millennium, the science centre includes hands-on exhibits and a planetarium (see page 94).

- **Scottish Football Museum** Everything you ever wanted to know about Scotland's contribution to the 'beautiful game' (see page 96).

- **Comedy Festival** One of Glasgow's annual highlights, as venues all over the town host international comedians (see page 12).

▼ *Kelvingrove Art Gallery*

Your at-a-glance guide to seeing the best Glasgow has to offer, depending on how much time you have.

HALF-DAY: GLASGOW IN A HURRY

If you're only in Glasgow on a business trip or just passing through but have time for a little exploration, head straight for the city centre quadrant of Buchanan Street and Argyle Street, where you can spend an hour or so in the Gallery of Modern Art (see page 68), indulge in some top class retail therapy in Princes Square (see page 76), then have a refreshing cup of tea in the wonderful Willow Tearooms (see page 77).

1 DAY: TIME TO SEE A LITTLE MORE

If you have more than half a day, head slightly east to take in the looming glory of Glasgow Cathedral (see page 64), soak up the atmosphere of Merchant City, once home to tobacco magnates and now a trendy area of bars and restaurants (see page 65), then enjoy the rambling atmosphere of The Barras market – a Glasgow institution (see page 72).

● *Glasgow Science Centre*

2–3 DAYS: SHORT CITY BREAK

With more time on your hands you will be able to take in several more aspects of this extensive city. Don't miss an opportunity to visit the Kelvingrove Art Gallery & Museum (see page 85), with one of the finest art collections in the country and, for a step back in time, visit the Museum of Transport (see page 85) to see how Glaswegians got around in days gone by. Head to the Southside of the city for the gleaming success that is the Glasgow Science Centre (see page 94) and take in the views of the Clyde riverbank, then take in the Burrell Collection (see page 98) and stroll around Pollok Park (see page 94).

LONGER: ENJOYING GLASGOW TO THE FULL

With added time you can either revisit some of the areas to take in more sights, such as the Glasgow School of Art with its Rennie Mackintosh designs (see page 70) or the historic Tall Ship on the Clyde (see page 97). But no one should miss the chance to get out into the countryside, particularly Loch Lomond (see page 118), one of the most picturesque areas of Scotland.

Something for nothing

Glasgow is not an expensive place to visit – at least no more so than any other British city. Additionally, many of the museums and galleries are free, although there may be charges for special temporary exhibitions.

When Glasgow was considerably expanded during the 19th century, the city planners had the foresight and consideration to include large pockets of greenery in their aims. As a result it has far more parks and gardens than the majority of cities that were created and developed during the Industrial Revolution. The Botanic Gardens (see page 82) are the highlight, but Pollock Country Park (see page 94) and Bellahouston Park (see page 92) also make for lovely strolls, providing the skies are clear. Should rain stop play when you are visiting Glasgow Green, you can duck into the People's Palace exhibition (see page 65) for a (free) potted history of the city. On the Southside, what was once a derelict industrial site has been transformed in recent years into the appropriately named Hidden Gardens. Their theme is spirituality and contemplation and the coming together of different faiths and cultures – the perfect place to escape Glasgow's bustle (ⓐ Albert Drive ⓣ 0141 433 2722 ⓦ www.thehiddengardens.org.uk).

The Victorians had a macabre fascination with death, and many 19th-century cemeteries are adorned with ornate neo-Gothic statuary. Glasgow's Necropolis (see page 64) has an abundance of florid mausoleums, tombs and gravestones. One can't help admire the skill of the sculptors and you can lose yourself for hours strolling around these flamboyant celebrations of past lives.

There's no better way to get an impression of Glasgow past and present than to stroll part of the Clyde Walkway. When the Clyde was still the centre of industry and shipbuilding this was a bustling area, and a few remnants of that time remain – such as the Finnieston Crane, which was used to lift large cargoes onto the ships. The Tall Ship (see page 97) and the Clydebuilt Scottish Maritime Museum (see page 99) also celebrate the past. Most uplifting, though, is to see how the area is being regenerated. The Glasgow Science Centre (see page 94), the Scottish Exhibition & Conference Centre (see page 96) and Pacific Quay are all part of this development, as is the Riverside Museum, still under construction but due to open in 2009.

⬤ *The People's Palace*

When it rains

Lucky indeed the visitor to Glasgow who doesn't experience a spot of wet weather. The city's rainy reputation is well founded and the likelihood is that you'll experience more than a few showers, if not a full-on downpour. Going out without an umbrella or a hat is foolhardy, to say the least.

That said, the city is also awash with fascinating museums that should keep you dry and enthralled for days. The Kelvingrove Art Gallery and Museum (see page 85) and the Burrell Collection (see page 42) both warrant several hours of attention, while the many buildings dedicated to Charles Rennie Mackintosh, such as the Glasgow School of Art (see page 70) and Mackintosh House in the Hunterian Art Gallery (see page 84), are must-sees that are also protected from the elements. Or why not keep dry with a warming cup of tea in the Mackintosh-designed Willow Tearooms (see page 77)? If you've got kids in tow, they will be absorbed for hours by the interactive exhibits at the Glasgow Science Centre (see page 94).

Partly because of the weather conditions, Glasgow is also very strong on shopping centres. The most elegant of these is Princes Square (see page 76) with its four floors of chic boutiques and ground floor cafés and restaurants. If you've got a bit more cash in your wallet and crave a European experience to combat the Scottish climate, don't miss the Italian Centre (see page 74), which brings a spot of Mediterranean sparkle to the grey skies.

Indoor sporting options include go-karting (☏ 0800 698 5278 ⊕ www.scotkart.co.uk). Or, if you're gastronomically inclined, the Glasgow Cookery School offers one-day courses on all manner of cuisines, including Scottish (ⓐ 65 Glassford Street ☏ 0141 552 5239 ⊕ www.thecookeryschool.org).

Of course, this being Scotland you're never more than a few steps from a pub, where a pint of ale and a hearty meat pie can do wonders to lift the spirits if the heavens have decided to open.

◆ *The Glasgow School of Art*

On arrival

TIME DIFFERENCES

Glasgow's clocks follow Greenwich Mean Time (GMT). During Daylight Saving Time (end Mar–end Oct) the clocks are put forward one hour. In the Scottish summer when it is noon in Glasgow, time at home is as follows:

Australia Eastern Standard Time 21.00, Central Standard Time 20.30, Western Standard Time 19.00
New Zealand 23.00
South Africa 12.00
USA and Canada Newfoundland Time 08.30, Atlantic Canada Time 08.00, Eastern Time 07.00, Central Time 06.00, Mountain Time 05.00, Pacific Time 04.00, Alaska 03.00

ARRIVING
By air

Glasgow International Airport (ⓦ www.baa.com/glasgow) is 12 km (8 miles) from the city centre and an efficient Air Link coach connects the two for the 20-minute journey. There are also plenty of taxis for a higher cost. There are daily flights between Glasgow and London and many other British cities, as well as flights to international destinations including Europe and the USA. There are also international flights from Glasgow Prestwick International Airport (ⓦ www.gpia.co.uk) which is 48 km (30 miles) from the city centre.

By rail

There are two main train stations in Glasgow: Central Station on Gordon Street serves trains to the south and west; Queen Street

Station on Dundas Street serves trains to the north and east. Train services into Glasgow are handled by the Great North Eastern Railway (GNER), Virgin and ScotRail. There are daily services between London and Glasgow making the 5-hour journey, as well as direct links to many other British cities. For timetables and fares contact National Rail Enquiries ☎ 08457 48 49 50 ⓦ www.nationalrail.co.uk

⬤ *Glasgow's Central Station*

Glasgow

0   200 metres
0   200 yards

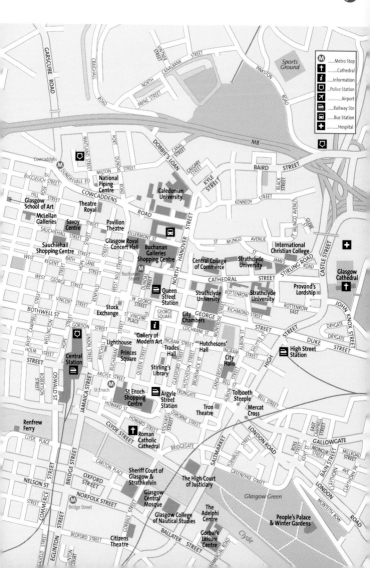

By bus

National Express coaches (☎ 08705 80 80 80
ⓦ www.nationalexpress.com) link Glasgow with various UK and
Scottish cities and is a great budget option for getting to the city.
The main bus station is Buchanan Bus Station on George Square.

Driving

The main motorway route into Glasgow is the M6/M74, which
travels up the west of England, through Cumbria. The city is directly
linked to Edinburgh via the M8. The journey time by road between
London and Glasgow is about 9 hours.

FINDING YOUR FEET

Glasgow is generally a safe city as long as you're in the central
tourist areas, so no visitor should feel any sense of threat, although
like everywhere, in crowded tourist spots pickpockets may be in
operation so keep an eye on your belongings at all times. Traffic can
be a problem in the centre so use the pedestrian crossings, wait for
the green man to light up, and remember that traffic will be coming
from the right (not the left). Policemen, taxi drivers and locals, who
have a well-founded reputation for being friendly, will all help if you
need to ask for directions.

ORIENTATION

Glasgow is a large city so it's best to arm yourself with a map,
available free from the tourist office (see page 153). The main areas
for tourists are the city centre, Merchant City, the West End and the
Southside. The central axis of the city centre are the interconnecting

---

▶ *A statue of one of Scotland's heroes, Robert the Bruce*

Sauchiehall, Buchanan and Argyle streets. Exploring on foot within each area is the best option, but for travelling around the bus service is excellent, the subway system links the city centre and the West End, and taxis are plentiful. There's also an extensive train network for more outlying districts.

GETTING AROUND

Buses

There is an extensive bus network in Glasgow operated by First buses (📞 0141 423 6600 🌐 www.firstgroup.com). Glass sheltered bus stops are in abundance and will have a plan of the route each numbered bus will take. Selected stops on the route are also written on the front of the bus. Single-day bus passes are available or you can pay for single fares, but you must have the exact change. A standard single fare in the city is currently 80 pence. The main bus station in Glasgow is on George Square in the city centre, from where you can take buses around the city, and to many other places around Scotland.

Subway

Glasgow's Subway SPT (Strathclyde Passenger Transport) is the third oldest subway system in the world. Single tickets or day or weekly passes can be bought at station ticket offices or, with the correct change, at the ticket machines. For more information contact SPT (📞 0141 332 6811 🌐 www.spt.co.uk).

Taxis

Black cabs are in plentiful supply on Glasgow's streets and can be hailed from the pavement if their yellow For Hire light is on. Most taxi drivers are friendly and helpful and love to talk about their city

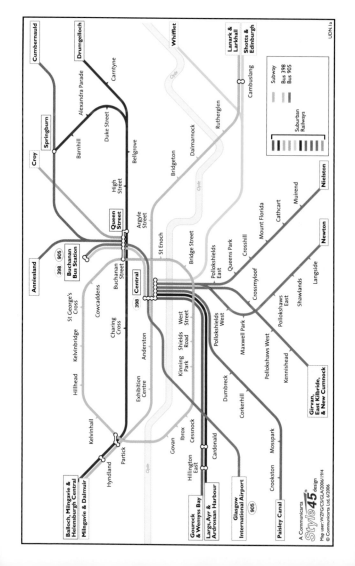

with tourists. Fares are metered and the cost is shown on a light above the driver's windscreen. At the end of your journey pay the driver through the glass cavity between the driver's and passenger's compartment. The limit of passengers per taxi is five people. There are also various companies that you can telephone to order a taxi from your location, including:

Glasgow Taxis ☎ 0141 429 7070
Online Radio Cars ☎ 0141 550 4040

DRIVING IN GLASGOW

❶ Traffic can be heavy in the city and parking is restricted, so driving is not the most sensible option. If you do want to drive, however, make sure you understand the parking regulations, use pay and display ticket machines or one of the multistorey car parks, and never park on double yellow lines or red routes. Traffic wardens abound and are very keen on writing tickets.

If you're just coming into Glasgow for the day, en route to other destinations, there is a useful 'Park and Ride' scheme, where you can park your car on the outskirts of the city and take a bus into the centre. Locations of the many 'Park and Ride' stops are indicated on the city's transport map, available from the tourist office, the bus station and mainline stations.

CAR HIRE

Hiring a car certainly isn't necessary if you are just going to explore the city. However, it can be a very convenient way to get around if you plan to visit outlying areas. As well as multinational chains such

▶ *The many bridges over the River Clyde make for an interesting walk*

as Avis and Hertz there are several Glasgow-based car hire options. Costs obviously vary between companies, but the average for an economy size car is £30 for a day and £150 for a week's hire.

Avis ☏ 0870 606 0100 ⓦ www.avis.co.uk
Clarkson of Glasgow ☏ 0141 771 3990 ⓦ www.carhirescotland.com
Hertz ☏ 0141 248 7736 ⓦ www.hertz.co.uk
Thrifty Car Rental ☏ 0141 848 5002 ⓦ www.thrifty.co.uk

🔽 *This ornate building is now the Travel Centre in St Enoch*

▶ *Kelvingrove Park*

City Centre & Merchant City

Glasgow's city centre may not have the trendy reputation of the West End on the other side of the M8 that cuts through the city, but it is where the action is in terms of its administration, businesses and high-street shopping. Glasgow was founded on the site of its cathedral, so this is the true heart of the city both historically and financially. Much of Glasgow's wealth emerged in the 18th and 19th centuries, when the import of tobacco from the New World created filthy rich magnates who built their homes and warehouses in the area now known as Merchant City. These glorious edifices have now been given over to shops and restaurants that have helped boost Glasgow's fortunes once again since the last decade of the 20th century.

SIGHTS & ATTRACTIONS

Celtic Football Club Visitor Centre & Museum

Football is the life blood of Glasgow, and anyone interested in the native Celtic club should pay a visit here. From its beginnings in 1888 the museum charts the triumphs and disappointments that are all part of the 'beautiful game' with displays of trophies and past teams, and there's also the chance to tour the stadium.
ⓐ Celtic Park ⓣ 0141 551 4308 ⓦ www.celticfc.net ⓛ tours daily (except match days) 11.00, noon, 13.45, 14.00. Admission charge

City Chambers

The 19th century was the heyday of Glasgow's history and this striking building reflects the success of the time with its marble staircases and frescoed ceilings. Glasgow City Council still operates

City Centre &
Merchant City

from behind the majestic façade, which dominates George Square.
ⓐ George Square ⓣ 0141 287 4018 ⓦ www.glasgow.gov.uk ⓛ Tours
10.30 & 14.30 Mon–Fri

Glasgow Cathedral & Necropolis

Dating from the 12th century, this is, quite rightly, one of the city's
most impressive buildings and is the lone mainland survivor of the
Scottish Reformation of the 16th century. Its most important feature
is the shrine of St Mungo, the first bishop of Strathclyde and the
patron saint of Glasgow. The Necropolis next to the cathedral only
dates from the 19th century but is full of Gothic-style mausoleums
for many Glasgow notables (including William Miller, author of the
children's nursery rhyme 'Wee Willie Winkie').
ⓐ Cathedral Square ⓣ 0141 552 6891 ⓦ www.historic-scotland.gov.uk
ⓛ 09.30–18.00 Mon–Sat, 13.00–17.00 Sun, Apr–Sept; 09.30–16.30
Mon–Sat, 13.00–16.00 Sun, Oct–Mar

Martyrs' School

When primary education became compulsory in the late 19th
century, the country was involved in a mass project of school
building. This school was one of Charles Rennie Mackintosh's earliest
works; nevertheless his distinctive style can still be seen in what was
built as a primary school in 1897, including the tiling and the
woodwork. Particularly impressive is the monochrome staircase.
Following conventions of the time there is a separate entrance for
boys and girls, and classrooms radiating out from the central hall.
Renovated in 1999 it is now used by the staff of Glasgow Museums.
ⓐ Parson Street ⓣ 0141 553 2557 ⓦ www.glasgowmuseums.com
ⓛ By appointment only 10.00–17.00 Mon–Thur & Sat, 11.00–17.00
Fri & Sun

Merchant City

A huge influence on the rise of Glasgow's fortunes in the 18th century was the importing of tobacco, and in this region of the city centre the great tobacco magnates built their warehouses and opulent homes. Like many industrial areas in Britain, the region fell into disrepair in the 20th century, but in the 1980s a rejuvenation programme was put in place to preserve the architecture and revive its fortunes. One of the most successful ventures was Ingram Square, where derelict warehouses were converted into chic apartments, shops and cafés. Other buildings of note in the area include Hutchesons' Hall (1802) on Ingram Street, the Greek Revivalist Sheriff Courts (1842), also on Ingram Street and now home to the Scottish Youth Theatre, the City Halls (1882) on Candleriggs, the original Tolbooth (1625) at The Cross, the Britannia Music Hall (1857) on Trongate where Cary Grant once performed, the Virginia Galleries (1819), the former Tobacco Exchange on Virginia Street, and the Corinthian (1841) at the top of South Frederick Street. So important is the area now to the city's history that Glasgow Council have put in place a Merchant City trail.

Ⓦ www.glasgowmerchantcity.net

People's Palace & Glasgow Green

Glasgow Green was a grazing land in medieval times and also served as a horse market – a history still commemorated by the annual Glasgow Fair held here each July. Within the green is a memorial to the inventor James Watt, who is said to have figured out his steam engine mechanisms while taking a stroll here. The People's Palace was opened in 1898 and is now home to a museum dedicated to Glasgow's history and its people – there are re-creations of a prison cell here, displays about Clyde steamers and, quirkily, the banana boots that comedian Billy Connolly wore during the documentary 'Big Banana Feet', which was to make his name. The glasshouse next door is home to an array of tropical plants as well as a café.

ⓐ Glasgow Green ❶ 0141 271 2951 ◐ 10.00–17.00 Mon–Thur & Sat, 11.00–17.00 Fri & Sun

Provand's Lordship

Since Glasgow burst into prominence during the Industrial Revolution, it's sometimes hard to remember that people were living here centuries beforehand. This, the only surviving medieval house in the city, is proof of its long history, dating from 1471. Inside is a collection of historic furniture and exhibitions detailing life in the city in the Middle Ages.

ⓐ Castle Street ❶ 0141 552 8819 ⓦ www.glasgowmuseums.com ◐ 10.00–17.00 Mon–Thur & Sat, 11.00–17.00 Fri & Sun

Tenement House

Tenement living is central to Glasgow's history, as much as it is to New York's. In this tenement building, one flat of four rooms has been preserved in the manner in which it was lived in by one resident for five decades from 1911 until 1965, detailing the history of tenement living and domestic life in the early 20th century. There's also a general exhibition on life in the tenements.

ⓐ Buccleuch Street ❶ 0141 333 0183 ⓦ www.nts.org.uk ◐ 13.00–17.00 Mar–Oct. Admission charge

◐ *Victorian statuary at the Necropolis*

Trades Hall

This lovely 18th-century building designed by the great architect Robert Adam was home to the trading body that was responsible for training craftsmen. Today it houses an audio exhibition on the history of the city, from medieval times to the present day.

@ Glassford Street @ 0141 552 2418 @ www.tradeshallglasgow.co.uk
@ 10.00–17.00 Mon–Fri, 10.00–14.00 Sat, noon–17.00 Sun, Apr–Oct; noon–17.00 Sun, Nov–Mar. Admission charge

CULTURE

Collins Gallery

Ten annual exhibitions are staged in the University of Strathclyde's gallery in all manner of contemporary genres – multimedia, applied art and installations have all been seen here. Workshops are also held here.

@ Richmond Street @ 0141 548 2558 @ www. collinsgallery. strath.ac.uk/ @ 10.00–17.00 Mon–Fri, noon–16.00 Sat

Gallery of Modern Art

If you were ever in doubt of the wealth of Glasgow's tobacco merchants, take a look at the façade of the Gallery of Modern Art – it was once the private residence of one such magnate. The building was then the city's Royal Exchange until it was converted into a wonderful art gallery in 1996. Focusing on contemporary art from the postwar period to the present day, among the artists featured are Damien Hirst and Grayson Perry.

◗ *Glasgow's Gallery of Modern Art*

📍 Queen Street ☎ 0141 229 1996 🌐 www.glasgowmuseums.com
🕐 10.00–17.00 Mon–Wed & Sat, 10.00–20.00 Thur, 11.00–17.00
Fri & Sun

Glasgow Police Museum
Glasgow was the first British city to have a police force and this
museum details its history from its beginnings in 1779. Truncheons,
handcuffs, uniforms, whistles, helmets and all manner of other
police paraphernalia are featured here. There is also an exhibition
dedicated to police uniforms from around the world.
📍 St Andrew's Square ☎ 07788 532691
🌐 www.policemuseum.org.uk 🕐 10.00–16.30 Mon–Sat, noon–16.30
Sun, Apr–Oct; 10.00–16.30 Tues, noon–16.30 Sun, Nov–Mar

Glasgow School of Art
Although this is still an ongoing learning institution bustling with
students hoping to be the next bright young thing on the art scene,
the importance of the building as a Charles Rennie Mackintosh
masterpiece means that guided tours are held here. Mackintosh
designed the building in 1896, including a façade that is dominated
by huge windows, bringing vast amounts of light into the art
studios. Inside is the beautiful wood-panelled library and collections
from the artist's body of work, including sketches and furniture.
📍 Renfrew Street ☎ 0141 353 4526 🌐 www.gsa.ac.uk 🕐 Tours
10.30–14.30 Apr–Sept; 11.00 & 14.00 Mon–Fri, 10.30 & 11.30 Sat,
Oct–Mar. Admission charge

The Lighthouse
The city's centre for architecture and design does, of course, include
a large exhibition on the life and work of Rennie Mackintosh, plus a

lot more besides. Touring exhibitions have included contemporary glassworks, retrospectives on Scottish architecture and emphasis on young designers. The Mackintosh tower offers great views of the city, as does the rooftop café.

ⓐ 11 Mitchell Lane ☏ 0141 221 6362 ⓦ www.thelighthouse.co.uk
🕓 10.30–17.00 Mon, Wed, Fri & Sat, 11.00–17.00 Tues, noon–17.00 Sun. Admission charge

McLellan Galleries

Built to house the art collection of a 19th-century Industrialist, the McLellan Galleries are now also home to constantly changing touring art exhibitions.

ⓐ Sauchiehall Street ☏ 0141 565 4137 ⓦ www.glasgowmuseums.com
🕓 10.00–17.00 Mon–Thur & Sat, 11.00–17.00 Fri & Sun

National Piping Centre

There's no sound quite so reminiscent of Scotland than the bagpipes, and this museum traces the history of the instrument and Highland music, with various sets of pipes from different periods. There's also a piping school where you can try your hand at playing the notoriously difficult instrument yourself in either day or evening classes.

ⓐ McPhater Street ☏ 0141 353 0220 ⓦ www.thepipingcentre.co.uk
🕓 09.30–16.30 Mon–Fri. Admission charge

Royal Highland Fusiliers Museum

Those interested in military history will have their fill here, as the museum records the history of the Scottish regiment through documents, uniforms and other military artefacts.

ⓐ Sauchiehall Street ☏ 0141 332 0961 ⓦ www.rhf.org.uk
🕓 09.00–17.00 Mon–Fri

St Mungo Museum of Religious Life and Art

St Mungo may be the Christian patron saint of Glasgow, but this museum celebrates tolerance by bringing together exhibits on the six major religious faiths of the world – Christianity, Judaism, Islam, Buddhism, Hinduism and Sikhism. There's even a Zen garden, extolling Buddhist harmony.

ⓐ Castle Street ❶ 0141 553 2557 ⓦ www.glasgowmuseums.com
ⓛ 10.00–17.00 Mon–Thur & Sat, 11.00–17.00 Fri & Sun

RETAIL THERAPY

The Barras One of the most authentic pockets of Glasgow, this indoor and outdoor market (see page 25) has an eclectic collection of knick-knacks, genuine antiques and, frankly, rubbish. But the atmosphere and the market characters are what makes this such a memorable experience. ⓐ Gallowgate

Buchanan Galleries One of Glasgow's newest shopping centres and proving a great success, not least for its location. Standard high-street stores such as Mango and Gap can be found here, as well as a branch of John Lewis. ⓐ 220 Buchanan Street ❶ 0141 333 9898 ⓦ www.buchanangalleries.co.uk

Fireworks Studios No rockets or Catherine wheels here – the fireworks refers to the process by which they produce original ceramic designs. The centre also runs pottery workshops if you want to try your hand at it yourself. ⓐ 35a Dalhousie Street ❶ 0141 332 3738 ⓦ www.fireworkstudio.co.uk

---

❶ *The Princes Square shopping centre has style both inside and out*

CHARLES RENNIE MACKINTOSH

No other architect or designer has had such an effect on Glasgow's landscape and in quite such an attractive manner as Charles Rennie Mackintosh. Born in the city in 1868, Mackintosh studied at the old Glasgow School of Art as well as working as an apprentice architect, and began to merge the two previously very different design forms into one. Taking inspiration from Art Nouveau and the Arts and Crafts movements that were sweeping across Europe and America, Mackintosh invoked Scottish symbolism into these forms with motifs such as his trademark rose. Other typical features of his design included the use of monochrome black and white colour schemes, high-backed geometric-shaped chairs and curved lamps. One of his most famous works, aside from the Glasgow School of Art, is the Willow Tearooms (see page 77). Commissioned by his unofficial patron Catherine Cranston, who wanted to open a new dining emporium, Mackintosh mixed grey silk with purple velvet, and adorned the elegant area with chandeliers and glass doors. He also installed a window the full width of the room – an unusual feature at the time. He died in London in 1928.

✓ **The Italian Centre** Italy has long been known as a leader in design, and this unique centre promotes the very best that the country has to offer in designer clothing and accessories, including branches of Armani and Versace. In addition there are plenty of cafés and bars if you want to rest your feet and ponder your purchases. ⓐ 7 John Street ⓣ 0141 552 6368

The Lighthouse If you're a design junkie, head to the gift shop of The Lighthouse gallery (see page 70), where iconic designs such as the iPod and well-known names such as Alessi and Marimekko are on sale.

Merchant Square Every Saturday, the square is home to a craft and designers market that is perennially popular with locals and visitors. ⓐ Candleriggs ⓑ 11.30–18.00 Sat

Orro Contemporary Jewellery In the heart of Merchant City this is a wonderful collection of modern jewellery from some of the world's best-known designers. ⓐ 12 Wilson Street ⓣ 0141 552 7888 ⓦ www.orro.co.uk

🔺 *Interior of the Merchant Square market*

Princes Square The most elegant place to shop in the city – with everything under one roof. Behind an innocuous looking façade, the interior opens out to reveal a four-storey emporium of upmarket shops and designer one-offs, fountains and restaurants.
🅐 48 Buchanan Street 🕿 0141 221 0324
🅦 www.princessquare.co.uk

St Enoch Shopping Centre This may be the largest glass building in Europe but the shopping centre within lacks any finesse. Still, it's good for families, with a play centre, and for picking up everyday items from high-street chains. 🅐 55 St Enoch Square 🕿 0141 204 3900 🅦 www.stenoch.co.uk

Slanj Kiltmakers If you're after a bit of traditional tartan or Highland gear, this is the place to come. 🅐 166 Hope Street 🕿 0141 248 7778 🅦 www.slanj.co.uk

TAKING A BREAK

Café Gandolfi ❶ A Merchant City favourite with a stunning interior of stained glass and wood. Snacks and more substantial dishes are both available. 🅐 64 Albion Street 🕿 0141 552 6813 🅦 www.cafegandolfi.com

Café Hula ❷ Home-made soup, enormous sandwiches and fresh cakes make this an ideal lunch spot in the city centre. 🅐 321 Hope Street 🕿 0141 353 1660

Fratelli Sarti ❸ Specialising in Tuscan cuisine, the café of this well-known deli has a superb selection of antipasti – ideal for a

lunchtime snack. ⓐ 42 Renfield Street ⓣ 0141 572 7000
ⓦ www.fratellisarti.com

Fresh ❹ If you want lunch on the move or just fancy a warming cup of soup, this takeaway café is a great Merchant City find.
ⓐ 51 Cochrane Street ⓣ 0141 552 5532

Willow Tearooms ❺ Charles Rennie Mackintosh's beautifully designed tearooms were originally opened in 1903 and have recently been refurbished. There are few more elegant and historic places to enjoy a slice of cake and a cup of tea in the heart of the city's shopping district. ⓐ 217 Sauchiehall Street ⓣ 0141 332 0521
ⓦ www.willowtearooms.co.uk ⓛ 09.00–17.00 Mon–Sat,
11.00–16.15 Sun

AFTER DARK

Babbity Bowster £ ❻ Set in a lovely 18th-century building by Robert Adam restored in the 1980s' regeneration of Merchant City, this is one of Glasgow's most perennially popular pubs. There's also a restaurant on the first floor, and a small hotel above that (see page 36). ⓐ 16 Blackfriars Street ⓣ 0141 552 5055

Dakhin £ ❼ Southern Indian curries are the speciality here in what many consider one of the best Indians in the city. ⓐ 89 Candleriggs
ⓣ 0141 553 2585

Pancho Villas £ ❽ Not far from The Barras is this colourful Mexican restaurant serving sizzling fajitas, tacos and nachos.
ⓐ 26 Bell Street ⓣ 0141 552 7737

Arta ££ ❾ Set in what was once the city cheese market, this elegant Mediterranean restaurant, with an emphasis on both Spanish and Italian cuisine, benefits from an interior courtyard and a large bar. There's also a club on the premises on Friday and Saturday nights. ❸ The Old Cheesemarket, 62 Albion Street ❶ 0141 552 2101 Ⓦ www.g1group.co.uk

Café Cossachok ££ ❿ Glasgow's only Russian restaurant has been drawing crowds for almost two decades. As well as Russian fare such as beef stroganoff and *pelemni* (a type of ravioli), there are more than 40 brands of vodka on offer and, on Sundays, traditional Russian folk music. In addition, the staff wear traditional costume and the décor is an eclectic mix of Russian knick-knacks. ❸ 10 King Street ❶ 0141 553 0733 Ⓦ www.cossachok.com

⬥ *For unusual décor with your oysters, try Rogano*

Corinthian ££ ⓫ Set in the old Corinthian building beneath a beautiful glass-domed ceiling, the cuisine here is predominantly Scottish, with dishes such as Ayrshire lamb and Grampian chicken, although there are some European and Asian influences too. There's also a piano bar and a nightclub on site.
ⓐ 191 Ingram Street ⓣ 0141 552 1101 ⓦ www.g1group.co.uk

Gamba ££ ⓬ If you're a lover of seafood this is one of the best Glasgow options. It gets busy so it's wise to book. ⓐ 225a West George Street ⓣ 0141 572 0899

✓ **Rogano ££ ⓭** The seafood menu, including oysters, is reflected in the décor of this well-known restaurant, decorated in the manner the luxury *Queen Mary* cruise liner. ⓐ 11 Exchange Place
ⓣ 0141 248 4055

The Buttery £££ ⓮ The oldest restaurant in Glasgow (est. 1856) set in an old tenement building doesn't rest on its laurels, and still serves excellent Scottish cuisine. You'd do well to dress smartly and book ahead. ⓐ 652 Argyle Street ⓣ 0141 221 8188

Etain £££ ⓯ Considered one of the best dining options in Glasgow, this Terence Conran venture is within the Princes Square shopping complex. British menu and local produce are the key.
ⓐ The Glasshouse, Springfield Court ⓣ 0141 225 5630

Windows £££ ⓰ Enjoy wonderful views of the city while dining on top-quality Scottish fare in the rooftop restaurant of the Carlton George Hotel. ⓐ 44 West George Street ⓣ 0141 354 5070
ⓦ www.carltonhotels.co.uk

The West End

The West End is the trendiest area of Glasgow today. However, until the middle of the 19th century there was little here at all bar a few mansions for the wealthy who appreciated the 'country' atmosphere. But the Industrial Revolution changed all that. With the city centre given over to enterprise it had also become unbearably crowded and dirty, and it was clear that land would have to be developed to house the growing number of residents of this burgeoning city. The formerly rural district to the west began to see a building boom of terraces and tenements, constructed from local sandstone, with particular care taken to ensure that parks and gardens, such as Kelvingrove, were also thrown into the mix. These were to be the new homes of the equally newly created middle classes.

Among the architects to contribute to this were Charles Rennie Mackintosh and Alexander 'Greek' Thomson, so named because of his love of the Greek Revival style, which earned Glasgow the title City of Architecture in 1999.

Because the M8 motorway cuts through the heart of the city, the West End still has a very separate feel to the bustling centre – bohemian, stylish and a far cry from the slightly rough and run-down image of Glasgow of old. The presence of the university here also means that there's a youthful buzz to the area almost year round. While most of the sights are clustered around the city centre, the West End is the place to come to shop, drink and people watch.

SIGHTS & ATTRACTIONS

Botanic Gardens

Originally intended as a private centre of learning and a place to grow botanic specimens for the science students of Glasgow University, the beautiful botanic gardens are now very much open to the public. The highlight is the vast glasshouse with a domed ceiling, which reopened in 2006 after extensive restoration. Inside are tropical plants that can only thrive in this northerly setting within the heated conditions inside. There's also a rose garden, a herb garden and a popular children's playing area.

ⓐ Great Western Road and Queen Margaret Drive ⓣ 0141 334 2422 ⓦ www.glasgow.gov.uk ⓖ Gardens: 07.00–dusk; Glasshouse: 10.00–16.45 Apr–Oct; 10.00–16.15 Nov–Mar

Fossil Grove

In 1887, during development of the land that is Victoria Park, 11 fossilised tree stumps were found here, which indicates that a forest existed here more than 300 million years ago. The tree species, giant clubmoss, is now extinct. Today the trees are protected in a specially constructed building but there is a viewing gallery and detailed explanations about the importance of the site.

ⓐ Victoria Park ⓣ 0141 287 2000 ⓦ www.glasgowmuseums.com ⓖ Noon–17.00 Nov–Mar. Admission charge

Mitchell Library

This vast public reference library, open to members and non-members, contains the largest collection of works by that beloved

▶ *The Botanic Gardens are open to the public*

Scottish poet Robert Burns, as well as numerous rare manuscripts, maps and documents. The library also regularly holds temporary art exhibitions.

ⓐ North Street ⓣ 0141 287 2999 ⓦ www.glasgow.gov.uk
ⓛ 09.00–20.00 Mon–Thur, 09.00–17.00 Fri & Sat

Ruchill Church Hall

Yet another of Charles Rennie Mackintosh's contributions to Glasgow, this mission hall still has a regular congregation of worshippers but art lovers are equally welcome.

ⓐ 15–17 Shakespeare Street ⓣ 0141 946 6600
ⓦ www.crmsociety.com ⓛ 11.00–15.00 Mon–Fri, Sept–June

CULTURE

Hunterian Art Gallery & Museum

After the Kelvingrove this is probably the best museum in Glasgow, originally put together via the collections of an 18th-century doctor William Hunter. Art lovers will have their fill here, with works by such masters as Rembrandt, Stubbs and Pissaro, as well as the largest collection of works by James McNeill Whistler outside the USA. There's also a significant collection of the Scottish Colourists and the art school known as the Glasgow Boys. However, the highlight of the gallery is the Mackintosh House, a reconstruction of Rennie Mackintosh's own abode on Florentine Terrace, put together from plans the architect drew up himself. The museum section features displays on zoology and anatomy, as well as collections exploring prehistoric life, ancient Egypt, the Romans and an area dedicated to the voyages of Captain Cook.

Gallery: ⓐ University of Glasgow, Hillhead Street ⓣ 0141 330 5431
Museum: ⓐ University of Glasgow, University Avenue ⓣ 0141 330
4221 ⓦ www.hunterian.gla.ac.uk ⓛ 09.30–17.00 Mon–Sat.
Admission charge to Mackintosh House

Kelvingrove Art Gallery & Museum

The highlight for Glasgow in 2006 was the re-opening of this
landmark gallery and museum after three intensive years of
refurbishment. Long the city's biggest draw for both locals and
visitors, this vast Edwardian building is home to a spectacular array
of art, including works by Van Gogh, Rembrandt, Botticelli and
Salvador Dalí's famous *Christ of St John on the Cross*. There's also a
vast weaponry collection, archaeological finds and natural history
items, and a restored Spitfire suspended from the ceiling. Displays
are arranged by themes within the 22 galleries.
ⓐ Kelvingrove ⓣ 0141 287 2699 ⓦ www.glasgowmuseums.com

Museum of Transport

The advances in transport in the 19th and 20th centuries were so
extraordinary that it seems every major city these days has a
museum dedicated to the subject. But this is certainly one of the
best, not least because Glasgow has a long history of being at the
forefront of shipbuilding, as well as railway and car manufacturing.
From horse-drawn carriages to Concorde, nothing is left unexplored
here, but for a real step back in time don't miss the re-created 1930s
street, complete with pub, café, bakery, an underground station and
cars appropriate to the time. The Clyde Room, meanwhile, explores
the city's highly important contribution to shipbuilding.
ⓐ Bunhouse Road ⓣ 0141 287 2720 ⓦ www.glasgowmuseums.com
ⓛ 10.00–17.00 Mon–Thur & Sat, 11.00–17.00 Fri & Sun

RETAIL THERAPY

Alba Second-hand Music A lovely speciality shop for budding musicians, Alba sells a vast range of second-hand sheet music for all manner of instruments. ⓐ 55 Otago Street ⓣ 0141 357 1795 ⓦ www.albamusick.co.uk

Bookpoint If you want to know more about Glasgow and Scotland in general this is the place of choice, stocking a wide range of titles dedicated to the subject. ⓐ 143 Hyndland Road ⓣ 0141 334 5522

Coach House Trust Shop The Coach House Trust Project endeavours to help people with mental health problems, both psychologically

🔺 *Kelvingrove Art Gallery & Museum is Glasgow's finest museum*

and economically through craft workshops, and the results of their efforts are on sale here. Wooden furniture, clocks, artworks and mosaic tables are all beautifully crafted and also quite unique.
📍 518 Great Western Road ☎ 0141 334 6888

Felix and Oscar Adult and children's wear, designer jewellery, unusual handbags and even kitchenware are all on sale in the eclectic boutique. You could spend hours browsing here.
📍 De Courcy's Arcade, Cresswell Lane ☎ 0141 339 0269

Galletly and Tubbs An eclectic range, from Italian ceramics to glass Buddhas to vegan handbags, have made this a hugely popular interior design store. 📍 431 Great Western Road ☎ 0141 357 1001

Go Potty If you love ceramics and want to try your hand at making your own, pop in here where experienced staff can teach you the basics. 📍 691 Great Western Road ☎ 0141 341 0520

I J Mellis A wonderful cheesemonger that features produce from around the world, but why go travelling when Scotland makes some of the best cheeses right on their doorstep? Also sells traditional accompaniments such as oatcakes. 📍 492 Great Western Road

JKJ Beautiful designer jewellery by the shop's owner Judith Kenny. She'll also be happy to take on commissions if you want a special piece made. 📍 9 Park Road ☎ 0141 334 0995

Pink Poodle A wonderful array of funky fashion created by a range of young designers. Certainly the place to come if you like standing out from the crowd. 📍 181 Byres Road ☎ 0141 357 3344

The Studio The West End is the best area in Glasgow for antique hunting, and The Studio is a treasure trove of genuine, well-sourced antiques. A speciality here is the Art Nouveau tiles, but there's also all manner of furniture, lamp shades, fire grates and books. ⓐ De Courcy's Arcade, Cresswell Lane
ⓣ 0141 334 8211

TAKING A BREAK

Hummingbird ❶ A lovely little coffee shop selling freshly baked organic bread, mouthwatering cakes and home-made soups.
ⓐ 59 Hyndland Street ⓣ 0141 334 9699

Jellyhill ❷ A relaxed but classy little café – an ideal place for a sandwich or salad lunch, or just a glass of wine. ⓐ 195 Hyndland Road ⓣ 0141 341 0055

Little Italy ❸ Part deli, part café, you can buy delicious panini and slices of pizza to go. ⓐ 205 Byres Road ⓣ 0141 339 6287

University Café ❹ This has been a West End institution since 1918 and, as its name would suggest, very popular with students. Its ice cream is legendary. ⓐ 87 Byres Road
ⓣ 0141 339 5217

AFTER DARK

The Bothy £ ❺ Scottish food at its hearty best – no frills here, just good honest cooking and delicious at that. ⓐ 11 Ruthven Lane
ⓣ 0141 334 4040

Café Andaluz £ ❻ A wonderful Spanish tapas restaurant
decorated in the Moorish style typical of Andalucia. Try fried chorizo
sausage in wine or spicy prawns or, for a larger meal, the traditional
Spanish paella. A great place to go with a group of friends, when you
can mix and match all the different dishes. ⓐ 2 Cresswell Lane
ⓣ 0141 339 1111

Café Royale £ ❼ Traditional Scottish fish and seafood, much of it
sourced from the Argyll coast where the owners also have a hotel
and restaurant. You can't get fresher than that, and it's great value
too. ⓐ 340 Crow Road ⓣ 0141 338 6606

Grassroots £ ❽ The best place in Glasgow for vegetarians –
international dishes and salads all served with flair that even
carnivores wouldn't turn down. ⓐ 97 St George's Road
ⓣ 0141 333 0534

Mother India £ ❾ One of Glasgow's best-known and best-loved
Indian restaurants – you should book ahead. Good choice for
vegetarians. There's a small wine list but you're also welcome to
bring your own. ⓐ 28 Westminster Terrace ⓣ 0141 221 1633

Stazione £ ❿ Housed in a former station ticket hall, yet despite
its Italian name the main influence on the menu here is Middle
Eastern cooking such as kebabs (on skewers not in bread) and
mezze. ⓐ 1051 Great Western Road ⓣ 0141 576 7576

Stravaigin £ ⓫ From Oriental-style duck to a traditional plate of
haggis, neeps and tatties (swede and mashed potato), Stravaigin
caters to all tastes. Its emphasis is on the freshest and most

seasonal produce – one of the reasons it's become a West End stalwart. @ 28 Gibson Street ☎ 0141 334 2665

Two Fat Ladies £ ⓬ If you're a fish lover you can't do much better than this. The restaurant has an excellent reputation of simply prepared fish and seafood, most of it locally sourced in Scotland, such as Loch Etive mussels. @ 88 Dumbarton Road ☎ 0141 339 1944

La Parmigiana ££ ⓭ Considered one of the best Italian restaurants in the country, which is quite a feat considering how many Italian restaurants there are in Glasgow. Seafood and game are the best options here, such as lobster ravioli. @ 447 Great Western Road ☎ 0141 334 0686

Loon Fung ££ ⓮ If it's popular with Chinese, then you know the food is good, and Loon Fung is always buzzing. The dim sum is excellent. @ 417 Sauchiehall Street ☎ 0141 332 1240

Òran Mor ££ ⓯ A lively place celebrating all that is great about Scottish culture, from food to music to whisky. @ 731 Great Western Road ☎ 0141 357 6226

Thai Fountain ££ ⓰ One of Glasgow's most popular Thai restaurants. As well as standards such as green curry, there are also specialities such as Volcano Chicken (chicken with Thai liqueur) and Pep Makham (duck in tamarind sauce). @ 2 Woodside Crescent ☎ 0141 332 1599

The Ubiquitous Chip £££ ⓱ Not only Glasgow's best-known restaurant, but one of the best known in Scotland. In 2005 it was awarded the 'Taste of Scotland' accolade, despite having been a landmark in the city for many, many years. Traditional Scottish fare might include Perthshire pigeon or Ayrshire lamb. ❸ 12 Ashton Lane ❶ 0141 334 5007

⬥ *For a lively evening, try Òran Mor*

Southside & River Clyde

For some 200 years Glasgow's Southside and the River Clyde were associated with shipbuilding and dockers and, like all port areas, had a rather shady atmosphere and reputation. When the shipbuilding stopped the area went into decline but, like so many dockland areas the world over that also witnessed this demise, the area has begun to see a regeneration in recent years. The opening of the Burrell Collection in 1983 brought visitors flocking over the river for the first time, and the area has rarely looked back since. Having overcome the shock that accompanied the end of the shipping industry, the city is now keen to celebrate what it once was and museums are dedicated solely to the subject. Meanwhile, taking advantage of cheaper rents than the West End, trendy shops, bars and restaurants have begun to move south, bringing to the area a new injection of style. Southsiders can, once again, be proud of their region.

SIGHTS & ATTRACTIONS

Bellahouston Park

One of Glasgow's many parks that emerged in the 19th century, created by city planners to counteract what would otherwise be an unstinting urban environment. The main feature of the park today, aside from the House for an Art Lover (see page 100), is its sporting facilities, including an 18-hole pitch and putt golf course and sports arena.

🄰 Dumbreck Road 🄣 0141 427 0558 🅦 www.glasgow.gov.uk.
🄻 Dawn–dusk

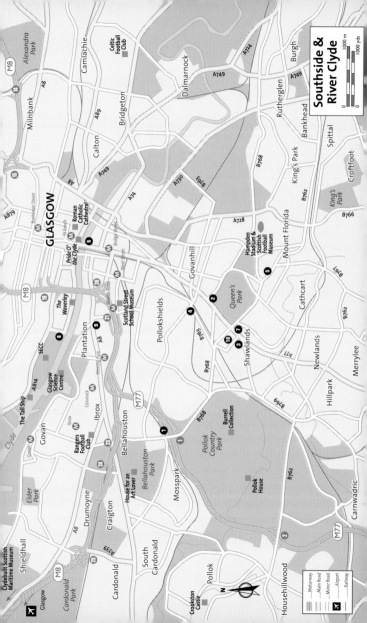

0   1000 m
0   1000 yds

Alexandra Park

M8

Milnbank

A8

Camlachie

Celtic Football Club

Bridgeton

A89

Dalmarnock

A724

Burgh

A749

Rutherglen

A749

Bankhead

Spittal

Croftfoot

Calton

A749

A8

A74

A739

B763

King's Park

B768

B762

Croftfoot

B766

GLASGOW

A879

Stockwell Street

Roman Catholic Cathedral

St Enoch

6

Pride O' the Clyde

West Street

Bridge Street

A728

Govanhill

Hampden Stadium & Scottish Football Museum

Mount Florida

King's Park

B766

The Waverley

M8

Eglinton Street

Scotland Street School Museum

9

7

Pollokshields

Queen's Park

5

Cathcart

B762

SECC

8

Plantation

A8

Kingston Road

B768

4

2

Shawlands

10

3

7

A77

Newlands

Merrylee

The Tall Ship

A814

Glasgow Science Centre

Ibrox

Bellahouston

B768

Pollok Country Park

Burrell Collection

B769

Hillpark

Clyde

Govan

Govan Road

Rangers Football Club

22

Bellahouston Park

1

B762

Clydebuilt Scottish Maritime Museum

Elder Park

24

House for an Art Lover

Mosspark

Pollok House

Carnwadric

Shieldhall

M8

Drumoyne

Craigton

A8

A739

South Cardonald

M77

Householdwood

Glasgow

Cardonald Park

Cardonald

Crookston Castle

Pollok

N

— Motorway
— Main Road
— Minor Road
✈ Airport
—— Railway

Crookston Castle

This part-ruined castle dates from the 14th century but fell into decline in the 15th century. Only one of its original four towers still survives, but it's all the more evocative for that.

ⓐ Brockburn Road ⓣ 0141 883 9606 ⓦ www.historic-scotland.gov.uk ⓛ 09.30–16.30 Apr–Sept; 09.30–16.30 Mon–Sat, 14.00–16.30 Sun, Oct–Mar

Glasgow Science Centre

Unlike London's disastrous Millennium Dome and wobbly Millennium Bridge, Scotland's year 2000 projects have been a success from the outset. The Glasgow Science Centre's gleaming structure of glass and steel is one of the best, with three floors of interactive exhibits exploring all manner of scientific advances, as well as a planetarium and an IMAX cinema. Its most popular feature, however, is its 127-m (416-ft) tower, which rotates 360 degrees. Weather permitting, visitors can take a glass lift to the top to gain one of the best panoramas of the city.

ⓐ Pacific Quay ⓣ 0141 420 5000 ⓦ www.gsc.org.uk ⓛ 10.00–18.00. Admission charge

Pollok House & Country Park

This graceful Georgian house and its surrounding park was home to the Maxwell family from 1750 until they donated it to the city in 1966. The exterior of the house is fronted by an impressive double staircase, while inside, past the marble hallway, there are artworks by the likes of Goya, William Blake and El Greco as well as countless pieces of antique furniture and ceramics. The servants' quarters are a wonderful insight into the running of the house in days gone by. Try to visit at the weekend when costumed staff bring this aspect 'to life'. The café is set in the original kitchen, complete with a cast-iron range. Aside from the Burrell Collection (see page 98) the park is dotted with walking trails, some of which can be undertaken accompanied by guides.

ⓐ 2060 Pollokshaws Road ⓣ 0141 616 6410 ⓦ www.nts.org.uk
ⓗ House: 10.00–17.00. Admission charge (free to park)

Pride O' the Clyde

Taking a ride on this waterbus along the Clyde is one of the best ways to see the Glasgow skyline from the river, including the Glasgow Science Centre, and a superb way to get a feel for how important the river is to the city through the guide's commentary.

● The Scottish Exhibition & Conference Centre is nicknamed the 'Armadillo'

📍 Departure points at Jamaica Street and Braehead Shopping Centre ☎ 07711 250969 🌐 www.clydewaterbusservices.co.uk
🕐 10.00–18.15. Admission charge

Rangers Football Club & Visitor Centre

Similar to the Celtic Football Club (see page 62), Rangers delights its fans by organising tours of its Ibrox Stadium including the players' dressing room and the press room. An exhibition gives a full history of the team and its numerous trophies are on display for all to see.
📍 Ibrox Stadium, Edmiston Drive ☎ 0870 600 1972
🌐 www.rangers.co.uk 🕐 Tours 11.00, 12.30, 14.30 Thur & Fri, 10.30 Sun. Admission charge

Scottish Exhibition & Conference Centre (SECC)

A packed annual calendar of events is held at the SECC, the largest exhibition centre in the city and a striking piece of silver architecture on the Clyde, nicknamed the 'Armadillo'. Big-name rock and pop stars stage concerts here, while exhibition areas stage large-scale events such as the Ideal Home Show.
☎ 0141 248 3000 🌐 www.secc.co.uk

Scottish Football Museum

Celtic and Rangers may have museums devoted entirely to their own teams, but here the full history of football throughout Scotland can be explored at the Hampden Stadium, the country's national football arena. There are 14 different themed exhibits, uncovering the history of the sport from its earliest days to modern times, as well as an international roll of honour and a Scottish Football Hall of Fame. A tour of the stadium includes visits to the dressing room, a chance to walk through the players' tunnel, visits to the presentation area and the Royal Box and even better, for boys young and old, the chance to kick a goal in the warm-up area.

ⓐ Hampden Park Football Ground, Aikenhead Road ⓣ 0141 616 6100 ⓦ www.scottishfootballmuseum.org.uk ⓛ 10.00–17.00 Mon–Sat, 11.00–17.00 Sun (except match days). Admission charge

The Tall Ship

Sadly, only five ships built on the Clyde in the long history of Glasgow's shipbuilding industry are still afloat, and this 1896 sample, the *sv Glenlee*, is one of them. A fuller account of the industry can be found at the Clydebuilt Scottish Maritime Museum (see page 99), but this is a far more evocative way to find out what life was like aboard ship and uncover the history through the eyes on a single vessel. Audio displays reproduce the sounds of sailors' voices, clinking chains and hauling ropes, the galley kitchen reveals the sparse and unappetising meals that were served, while the cargo hold reveals details of what was imported and exported on the often long journeys.

ⓐ Glasgow Harbour, Stobcross Road ⓣ 0141 222 2513 ⓦ www.thetallship.com ⓛ 10.00–17.00 Mar–Oct; 11.00–16.00 Nov–Feb. Admission charge

The Waverley

For decades the great Glaswegian annual tradition was to take a boat trip 'doon the watter' for their holidays, usually to the nearby islands of Bute and Arran. *The Waverley* paddlesteamer is a remnant of those days, and today visitors can take day or half-day cruises down the Firth of Clyde.

ⓐ Departures from Andersons Quay ⓣ 0845 130 4647 ⓦ www.waverleyexcursions.co.uk. ⓛ Apr–Oct. Admission charge

CULTURE

Burrell Collection

Like so many other 19th- and early 20th-century wealthy industrialists, shipping heir Sir William Burrell used his vast fortune to indulge his passion for art, eventually amassing more than 9,000

⬥ *Find out what life was like on board an original Tall Ship*

pieces from all over the world – including China and Egypt. European masters featured in the collection include Rembrandt and the famous *The Thinker* sculpture by Auguste Rodin. Burrell donated his collection to the city in 1944, but it wasn't until 1983 that the full works were opened to the public – not least because Burrell had stipulated that a gallery should be sited away from the pollution of the city centre. Pollok Park (see page 94) was donated to the city in the 1960s and finally provided a perfect setting to meet the collector's demands. Today the Burrell Collection is one of the most respected and popular in Britain.

ⓐ Pollok Country Park, Pollokshaws Road ⓣ 0141 287 2550
ⓦ www.glasgowmuseums.com ⓛ 10.00–17.00 Mon–Thur & Sat, 11.00–17.00 Fri & Sun

Clydebuilt Scottish Maritime Museum

Shipbuilding on the Clyde was one of the greatest mainstays of the Glasgow economy – some of the world's greatest liners, including the *QE2*, were built in here – until its final decline in the 1970s due to advances in transport and lack of demand. However, many still feel that it is an essential part of the Glasgow 'story', and this museum dedicates itself to the subject. With the aid of audiovisual displays, visitors are taken through the whole history from the 18th to the 20th century and are able to witness every stage in the process of building a ship, from first nail to inaugural launch. There's also much information about the importing of tobacco that made Glasgow rich, and later the trade in cotton – both benefits from possession of the New World in the 18th century. Kids in particular will also love the interactive exhibits that allow them to 'navigate' a ship and become trader for a day.

ⓐ Braehead ⓣ 0141 886 1013 ⓦ www.scottishmaritimemuseum.org
ⓛ 10.00–17.30 Mon–Thur & Sat, 11.00–17.00 Sun. Admission charge

House for an Art Lover

With plenty of original Charles Rennie Mackintosh buildings to see in the city, this reconstruction may seem a little unnecessary, but nevertheless it gives another fascinating insight into the architect and designer's visions. Built in the 1990s, it used plans and sketches drawn up by Mackintosh himself in 1901 for a house he intended to build as part of a design competition, but he was disqualified because he submitted his work too late. The re-created rooms also display the original illustrations so visitors can compare and contrast art versus life. For anyone fond of Mackintosh's designs, the gift shop is a treasure trove of gifts and jewellery using his trademark motifs.

ⓐ Bellahouston Park, Dumbreck Road ⓣ 0141 353 4770
ⓦ www.houseforanartlover.co.uk ⓛ 10.00–16.00 Mon–Wed, 10.00–13.00 Thur–Sun, Apr–Sept; 10.00–13.00 Sat & Sun, Oct–Mar. Admission charge

Scotland Street School Museum

The appeal here is two-fold: the architectural design of Rennie Mackintosh in this turn-of-the-century building; and the excellent internal exhibition detailing the history of 500 years of schooling in the city. The exhibits detail education from the 15th century onwards, but it is the re-creation of 19th- and early 20th-century classrooms and playgrounds that provides the most fascinating part of the museum and reveals how rapidly teaching methods, uniforms and discipline have changed within those 100 years.

ⓐ 225 Scotland Street ⓣ 0141 287 0500
ⓦ www.glasgowmuseums.com ⓛ 10.00–17.00 Mon–Thur & Sat, 11.00–17.00 Fri & Sun

RETAIL THERAPY

Braehead Shopping Centre Near the Clydebuilt Maritime Museum, this shopping centre has more than 100 outlets of the usual chains such as Gap and Next, as well as an ice-skating rink and children's play area. ⓐ Kings Inch Road ⓣ 0141 885 4600 ⓦ www.braehead.co.uk

The Candle Store All manner of candles, from the thick white church types to scented varieties, have been produced here since 1897. There's also a factory seconds area and tours to see the process of candlemaking in action. ⓐ 23 Robert Street ⓣ 0141 425 1661

Mithril Jewellery Both Celtic and art nouveau-inspired jewellery are the speciality here, all designed by owner Russell Caldwell. ⓐ 38 Battlefield Road ⓣ 0141 636 9366

Moon Guitars Any budding Hendrix or Clapton should make a stop here for its vast array of both acoustic and electric guitars. ⓐ 974 Pollokshaws Road ⓣ 0141 632 9526

TAKE A BREAK

Art Lover's Café ❶ As part of the House for an Art Lover (see page 99), the bright and airy café is a wonderful lunch or tea stop, decorated with a changing display of works by Scottish artists. ⓐ 10 Dumbreck Road ⓣ 0141 353 4779

Brooklyn Café ❷ Pasta, pizza, salads and delicious desserts are perfect for a quite substantial lunch. ⓐ 21 Minard Road ⓣ 0141 632 3427

Jam ❸   One of the newest cafés and restaurants that is helping to turn Southside into the city's hotspot. Decorated in retro style, coffee and sandwiches are served all day. ⓐ 28 Kilmarnock Road ❶ 0141 649 0944

Mise en Place ❹   Also a restaurant in the evening, this is a lovely place for a light lunch, serving pasta, crêpes, fish cakes and more. ⓐ 122–124 Nithsdale Road ❶ 0141 424 4600

AFTER DARK

Restaurants

Ali Shan £ ❺   Specialists in Indian and Pakistani dishes, with plenty to choose from if you're vegetarian. ⓐ 250 Battlefield Road ❶ 0141 632 5294

Salsa £ ❻   Near Glasgow Bridge this cheerful Mexican venue is more a bar than a restaurant, but does serve tasty staples such as tortillas. ⓐ 63 Carlton Place ❶ 0141 420 6328

Urban Grill £ ❼   Scottish dishes with a slight American and oriental influence from the chefs who made their mark at Gamba (see page 79). ⓐ 61 Kilmarnock Road ❶ 0141 649 2745

Yen £–££ ❽   A mix of all things oriental here. Upstairs is the cheaper noodle-style bar, while downstairs you can experience a traditional Japanese *teppanyaki* menu consisting of eight courses. ⓐ 28 Tunnel Street ❶ 0141 847 0110

La Fiorentina ££ ⑨ Specialising in Tuscan cuisine and with a wine list of more than 150 choices, this is one of the area's most popular Italian offerings. Try the delicious trio of monkfish, lobster and king prawns. ⓐ 2 Paisley Road West ⓣ 0141 420 1585 ⓦ www.le-fiorentina.com

▲ An old paddlesteamer, The Waverley offers cruises down the Firth of Clyde

Tusk ££ ❿ Set in a converted cinema and decorated with a 10-metre (30-foot) Buddha statue, huge draping curtains and a long mahogany bar. The menu has an Oriental influence, such as beef teriyaki, but there are also staple favourites such as fish and chips. One of the most stylish places on the Southside. ⓐ 18 Moss-Side Road ⓣ 0141 649 9199

Pubs & bars

Brechin's Set in a listed building, this pub once served shipyard workers and is now popular among Rangers supporters, whose stadium is nearby. Don't think of turning up here wearing green! ⓐ 803 Govan Road

Clutha Vaults A dark, albeit no longer smoke-filled Victorian pub, complete with snugs. Live music at the weekends. ⓐ 167 Stockwell Street ⓣ 0141 552 7520

The Old Toll Bar Lovely Victorian pub decorated with a marble bar, leather seats and opulent mirrors. There's also a restaurant downstairs. ⓐ 1–3 Paisley Road West ⓣ 0141 429 3135

Scotia Bar Tudor-beamed pub, popular with poets and folk and blues musicians. Claims to be the city's oldest pub although this isn't proven. ⓐ 112 Stockwell Street ⓣ 0141 552 8681

Victoria Bar Although it once served the fishmarket, the Victoria is now most popular on Friday nights when live folk music is played. ⓐ 157 Bridgegate

---

❿ *Balloch Castle is set in a country park at the southern end of Loch Lomond*

Clyde Valley

Rising in the border hills south of the city, the River Clyde flows through Glasgow and the heartland of industrial Scotland on its way to the Irish Sea. Along its banks are industrial and rural heritage sites, medieval castles, modern purpose-built visitor attractions, and some of southern Scotland's most attractive scenery, with landscaped parks, waterfalls and wooded glens where peregrine falcons nest. One of Scotland's busiest highways, the M74 motorway, passes through the region en route to Carlisle and northern England, yet surprisingly few visitors detour from the main road to explore the rich hinterland of the Clyde Valley. Despite its coal-mining and iron-smelting past, the region is full of opportunities to get away from the buzz of the city, with a plethora of country parks and wildlife reserves offering gentle strolls or longer walks in woodland parks and along the banks of the Clyde and its tributary streams and rivers.

GETTING THERE

There are trains from Glasgow Central to East Kilbride, Hamilton, Motherwell, Lanark and Paisley. Buses travel from

TOURIST OFFICES
Hamilton Tourist Information Centre ⓐ RoadChef Services, M74 (northbound), Hamilton ⓣ 01698 285590
Lanark Tourist Information Centre ⓐ Horsemarket, Ladyacre Road, Lanark ⓣ 01555 661661
Paisley Tourist Information Centre ⓐ 9a Gilmour St, Paisley ⓣ 0141 889 0711

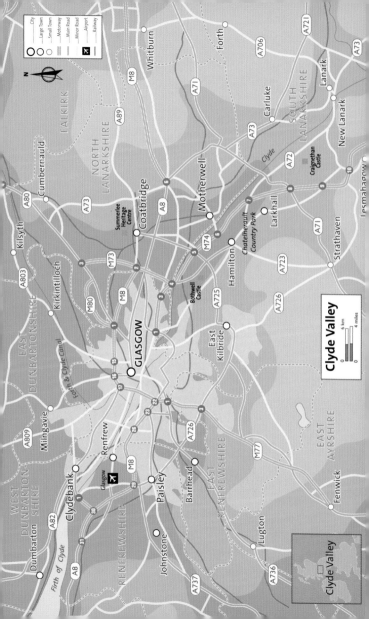

St Enoch Centre, Glasgow to all points in Lanarkshire and
Renfrewshire.

SIGHTS & ATTRACTIONS

Bothwell Castle

Overlooking the River Clyde, this dramatic 13th-century ruin was the
seat of the Black Douglases, allies of Robert the Bruce, and the most
powerful dynasty in these parts during the Middle Ages. It is one
of the largest and most striking of Scotland's early castles and is
a real slice of brooding, atmospheric history just a few kilometres
from the city centre.

🚌 24 km (15 miles) east of Glasgow at Uddingston, off the B7071
☎ 01698 816894 🌐 www.historic-scotland.gov.uk
🕐 10.00–17.00 Apr–Sept; 10.00–15.00 Sat–Wed, Oct–Mar.
Admission charge

Chatelherault Country Park

This outstanding grand hunting lodge and its walled gardens are all
that remain of one of Scotland's greatest aristocratic estates, the
seat of the wealthy and powerful dukes of Hamilton. An even
grander ducal palace was abandoned and demolished in the 1920s
after extensive mining undermined its foundations, but this
graceful pink sandstone building, designed by William Adam and
built in 1732, survived and was restored during the 1980s. Its
manicured gardens and grand salons are popular wedding and
reception venues, and it is surrounded by vast grounds where white
cattle roam and centuries-old oak trees – some more than 500 years

◀ *The formal garden at Chatelherault*

old – flourish. The River Avon flows through the grounds, and there are several guided walks, as well as a visitor centre that illustrates the history and natural heritage of the estate.

ⓐ Ferniegair, 2.5 km (1.4 miles) southeast of Hamilton on A72
ⓘ 01698 426213 **ⓛ** Visitor Centre: 10.00–17.00 Mon–Sat, noon–17.00 Sun; House: 10.00–16.30 Mon–Thur, noon–16.30 Sun

Craignethan Castle

Built in 1530 by Sir James Hamilton of Finnart, Craignethan is a rare example of a castle purpose-built to withstand bombardment by cannon, with a vaulted stone caponier or bunker, a sturdy residential tower and landscaped gardens.

ⓐ Off the A72, 1 km (0.5 miles) north of Crossford village
ⓘ 01555 860364 **ⓦ** www.historic-scotland.gov.uk **ⓛ** 10.00–17.00 Apr–Sept; 10.00–16.00 Sat–Wed, Oct; 10.00–15.00 Sat & Sun, Nov–Mar. Admission charge

Museum of Scottish Country Life

East Kilbride, where this museum is located, is a functional, purpose-built 'new town' on Glasgow's southern outskirts, created during the 1960s. The museum, an annex of the National Museum of Scotland (in Edinburgh), was built around a working farm and there is a collection of buildings, animals and farming equipment that show how the land was farmed during the first half of the 20th century. The farm and its Georgian farmhouse were the property of generations of the Reid family since the 16th century, and were donated to the National Trust for Scotland in 1992. The museum also has a year-round calendar of events, ranging from classic car and heavy horse shows to country fairs and collectors' events.

⊙ Wester Kittochside, Philipshill Road, East Kilbride ☎ 0131 247 3477
🕐 10.00–17.00. Admission charge

Hunter House Museum

Also in East Kilbride is the Hunter House Museum, the birthplace
of two luminaries of 18th-century Scotland, the brothers John
and William Hunter. An interactive exhibition describes their
achievements in medicine and science.

⊙ Maxwelltown Road, East Kilbride ☎ 01355 261261 🕐 12.30–16.30
Mon–Fri, noon–17.00 Sat & Sun, Apr–Sept

Motherwell Heritage Centre

An important centre of the iron and steel industry until the 1950s,
Motherwell has begun to reinvent itself as a centre of excellence
for the knowledge economy – but in many ways it's little more
than a suburb. Its chief attraction is the stunning Motherwell
Heritage Centre. This remarkable, space-age building opened in
1996 and is one of Scotland's most striking modern museums,
with a viewing platform that offers sweeping views of the valley
of the River Clyde, a Technopolis interactive display that follows
the area's history from the days of the Roman legions through to
the 19th-century heyday of the Age of Steam to the present day.
There's also an excellent foyer gallery with a changing programme
of exhibitions.

⊙ 1 High Road, Motherwell ☎ 01698 251000 🕐 10.00–17.00 Thur,
10.00–19.00 Wed & Fri & Sat, noon–17.00 Sun

Amazonia

Just outside Motherwell (off junction 5 of the M74 motorway),
Amazonia is one of Scotland's biggest indoor attractions, with exotic

plants and animals – including scorpions, bats, snakes, lizards and cute marmosets – in an artificial rainforest environment.

ⓐ Strathclyde Country Park, Motherwell ☎ 01698 333777

🕒 10.00–17.30. Admission charge

New Lanark World Heritage Village

This impressive beacon of enlightened capitalism was built in the late 18th century and founded by a Scottish industrialist, David Dale (1739–1806). Under the management of Dale's son-in-law, Robert Owen (1771–1858), the water-powered cotton mills employed more than 2,000 workers who were given decent housing, fair wages, free health care, training and schooling – including the world's first

🔺 *Robert Owen's utopian village, New Lanark*

nursery school – within the first ever properly planned industrial community. Although the last weaving mills closed in 1962, New Lanark has been restored and preserved as a living community with an award-winning visitor centre, working cotton-weaving machinery, and interactive displays that tell the story of the community and its visionary founder. At a time when most mill owners had little or no concern for the welfare of their workers, Owen's benevolent system was no less than revolutionary – and was regarded with some suspicion by his contemporaries.

🄰 New Lanark Visitor Centre, 2 km (1 mile) south of Lanark
🅘 01555 661345 🕒 10.30–17.00 June–Aug; 11.00–17.00 Sept–May. Admission charge

Scottish Wildlife Trust

The Clyde, which powered New Lanark's mills, flows through the village and upstream is the Scottish Wildlife Trust's Falls of Clyde Wildlife Reserve, with several kilometres of well-kept paths along the river and through wooded gorges where rare peregrine falcons nest in spring and early summer. There is a hide from which you can watch the peregrines' nest without disturbing the adult birds or their chicks. The river also attracts kingfishers, buzzards, dippers and other birds, as well as otter and deer.

🄰 Scottish Wildlife Trust Visitor Centre, New Lanark 🅘 01555 665262
🕒 11.00–17.00 Mar–Dec; noon–16.00 Jan & Feb. Admission charge

Paisley Abbey

This former weaving town, just south of Glasgow Airport, is now a residential suburb of Glasgow, with a handful of sights of its own. Most important is Paisley Abbey, with its medieval carvings, 14th–15th-century nave and colourful stained glass. King Robert III's

tomb is in the choir, and the abbey also contains the ancient Barochan Cross, dating from the dawn of Celtic Christianity. Founded in 1163 by Cluniac monks, the church was partly destroyed during the Reformation and was restored during the 19th century.
ⓐ Abbey Close, Paisley ⓣ 0141 889 7654 ⓛ 10.00–1530 Mon–Sat; services at 11.00, 12.15 and 18.30 on Sun

Paisley Museum

Paisley is also famous as the home of the colourful 'Paisley shawls', woven from fine wool in patterns copied from the traditional styles of northern India. Many of these beautiful shawls are on show in the Paisley Museum, in the town centre, which also has an excellent collection of pottery and 19th-century Scottish landscapes and portraits. Paisley also claims to be the birthplace of the great 14th-century Scottish patriot, William Wallace, and a 19th-century monument at Elderslie, south of the town centre, commemorates him.
ⓐ High St, Paisley ⓣ 0141 889 3151 ⓛ 10.00–17.00 Tues–Sat, 14.00–17.00 Sun

Summerlee Heritage Centre

This huge centre celebrates Lanarkshire's industrial heritage, with working machinery from vanished local industries, an old-fashioned tramway and a re-created coal mine with a row of typical mine-workers' cottages, all built on the site of a 19th-century ironworks.
ⓐ Heritage Way, Coatbridge, 24 km (15 miles) east of Glasgow centre
ⓣ 01236 431261 ⓛ 10.00–17.00 Apr–Oct; 10.00–16.00 Nov–Mar

▶ *The Scottish Wildlife Trust's Falls of Clyde*

ACTIVITIES

Calderglen Country Park

Here you can take country walks along the River Calder and its waterfalls. The park also has a visitor centre, children's zoo and an adventure playground. ⓐ South of East Kilbride on A726 ⓣ Visitor centre 01355 236644 ⓛ Dawn–dusk

Dollan Aqua Centre

In the centre of East Kilbride, this wet and wild leisure centre has a huge 50-m pool with water slides and play area. ⓐ Town Centre Park, East Kilbride ⓣ 01355 260000 ⓛ 7.30–22.00 Mon–Fri, 08.00–17.00 Sat & Sun. Admission charge

Forth & Clyde Canal Cruises

Narrowboat day trips on the Forth & Clyde Canal, which was built in 1790 and is gradually being restored, make for a pleasant day out. ⓐ Forth & Clyde Canal Society, Bishopbriggs, Glasgow ⓣ 0141 772 1620

James Hamilton Heritage Park

This country park on the outskirts of East Kilbride has a sailing loch with dinghies and sailboards for hire, as well as pedaloes, kayaks, canoes and rowing boats. ⓐ Stewartfield Way, East Kilbride ⓣ 01355 276611 ⓛ Apr–Oct

Strathclyde Country Park

With 1,000 acres of park and woodland surrounding a man-made lake, Strathclyde Country Park is Scotland's most popular open-air activity centre, offering sailing, boating, canoeing, parascending and cycling.

It even has its own beach. Equipment can be hired for all activities. Within the park is M & D's, Scotland's biggest theme park (☎ 0870 112 3777). ❷ Midway between Motherwell and Hamilton, off M74 (junction 5), 16 km (10 miles) south of Glasgow. ◷ Park: dawn–dusk; Water sports centre: 08.00–20.00. Park and visitor centre free; admission charge for water sports centre

AFTER DARK

Cricklewood £ Brasserie-style restaurant in residential suburb near Bothwell Castle. Open-air tables in summer. ❷ 27 Hamilton Road ☎ 01698 853172

Lanark Steayban £ Village pub-restaurant with an above-average menu. ❷ Glassford, near Lanark ☎ 01357 523400

Valerio's £ Classic fish and chip restaurant and diner in the centre of Lanark (5 minutes from New Lanark). Open all day. ❷ Bannatyne St, Lanark ☎ 01555 665818

La Vigna ££ Surprisingly good, classic Italian restaurant in Lanark, handily close to New Lanark. Open lunch and dinner. Good wine list. ❷ 40 Wellgate, Lanark ☎ 01555 664320

Trattoria Da Mario ££ Very good Italian trattoria. ❷ Strathaven, near Lanark ☎ 01357 522604

Loch Lomond & The Trossachs National Park

Glasgow's urban tentacles spread more than 16 km (10 miles) north and west of the city. But then there's a sharp change in the scenery as city streets and suburbs give way to wooded river valleys, rolling moorlands and hills, and the broad expanse of Loch Lomond, with its yachts, cruisers and dozens of tiny islands. Designated as Scotland's first national park in 2001, it covers 1,865 sq m (720 sq miles) and embraces wild open spaces in the Trossach hills, lonely medieval castles, pretty villages and gentle glens, with more than 50 rivers offering fine trout fishing. There are also more than 20 smaller lochs as well as the 'inland sea' of Loch Lomond – and it's all on Glasgow's doorstep. This part of the world is associated with two of Scotland's most famous heroes (or anti-heroes, if you come from south of the Border): William Wallace (1272–1305), Guardian of Scotland in the independence struggle of the early 14th century, and the outlaw, cattle-thief, Jacobite rebel and all-around swashbuckler Rob Roy McGregor (1671–1734), both of whom reputedly took refuge from their English pursuers in the woods and glens of the Trossachs. Wallace was, of course, eventually captured and gorily executed. Rob, on the other hand, was pardoned for his offences in 1725 and died in his bed at 63 – not a bad innings, considering his chosen career.

GETTING THERE

There are buses to Dumbarton, Balloch and Luss from Buchanan Bus Station in Glasgow city centre. These are operated by **First** (☎ 0141 423 6600 🌐 www.firstgroup.com). There are also **Scottish**

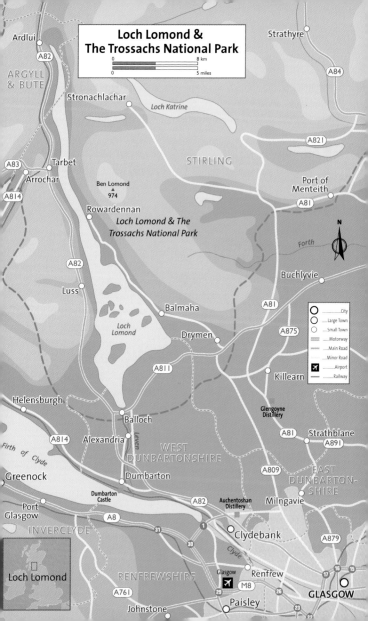

Citylink Coaches (☎ 08705 50 50 50) and **Strathclyde Passenger Transport services** (☎ 0141 332 6811 ⓦ www.spt.co.uk). By car, follow the M8/A82 west to Balloch via Dumbarton and Alexandria.

> **TOURIST OFFICE**
> Argyll, the Isles, Loch Lomond, Stirling and Trossachs Tourist Board ⓐ 7 Alexandra Parade, Dunoon ☎ 08707 200 269 ⓦ www.visitscottishheartlands.com

SIGHTS & ATTRACTIONS

Auchentoshan Distillery Visitor Centre

On the way to Loch Lomond (just off the A82), Auchentoshan is the closest distillery to Glasgow and is the only malt distillery in Scotland to triple-distil its malt in traditional copper pot stills. You can learn about the whole process, from malting to the final product – and sample a dram or two at the end of the tour.
ⓐ Dalmuir, Clydebank ☎ 01389 878561 ⓦ www.auchentoshan.com
🕒 Guided tours: 10.00–16.00 Mon–Sat. Admission charge

Balloch

At the southern end of Loch Lomond, Balloch is the starting point for cruises around the loch and its island and is a popular angling, sailing and water sports centre, with several marinas, a handful of pubs and restaurants, and a plethora of places to stay.

Balloch Castle Country Park

Balloch Castle Country Park, bordering the national park, was once the estate of one of medieval Scotland's most influential noble families. The small castle is more modern than it looks, dating as it does from the 19th century, and it now houses a visitor centre. Balloch's 80-hectare (200-acre) expanse of landscaped, wooded gardens is gradually being restored.

ⓘ 01389 722600 ⓦ www.lochlomond-trossachs.org ⓛ Country park: 24 hrs year round; Visitor centre: 10.00–17.00 Easter–Oct

Ben Lomond

Ben Lomond, 974 m (3,163 ft) above sea level, is the most prominent summit in the national park but is an easy enough hike, with the softest route starting from Rowardennan village on the east side of the loch. Allow at least six hours for the walk to the top and back, and bring good boots and waterproof outerwear.

Dumbarton

Dumbarton, on the north shore of the Clyde, is the gateway to Loch Lomond. Now a dormitory suburb of Glasgow, it was a famous shipbuilding centre during the 19th century and in even earlier times was the capital of two Dark Age kingdoms.

Dumbarton Rock & Castle

Dumbarton Rock, a 76-m (250-ft) high crag, has been fortified for at least 2,000 years. In the 5th and 6th centuries AD it was the capital of the kingdom of the Britons of Strathclyde and later became the seat of the earliest Scottish kings, who made it their capital until 1018, when they relocated to Dunfermline on the Firth of Forth. Today, the battlements and cannon of Dumbarton Castle, dating from the 18th and 19th centuries, still dominate the rock. Within is a 12th-century gateway, a gloomy dungeon and a sundial presented to the keepers of the castle by Mary, Queen of Scots.

🚇 Castle Road, Dumbarton ☎ 01389 732167 🌐 www.historic-scotland.gov.uk 🕐 9.30–18.30 Mon–Sat, 14.00–18.30 Sun, Apr–Sept; 9.30–18.30 Mon–Sat, 14.00–16.30 Sun, Oct–Mar. Admission charge

Glengoyne Distillery

In the Campsie Fells (the foothills of the Trossachs), the Glengoyne Distillery has been making fine single malt whiskies since 1833. Drawing its water from a 15-m (50-ft) high waterfall nearby, Glengoyne, with its whitewashed walls and slate roofs, is one of Scotland's most picturesque distilleries and is one of the few that still distil distinctive single malt whiskies in this part of the country. There are conducted tours of the still rooms and vaulted cellars, culminating in a sampling of Glengoyne's fine malts in a stylish reception room with views of the falls and the glen.

🚇 30 minutes from Glasgow on A81, south of Killearn village ☎ 01360 550254 🌐 www.glengoyne.com 🕐 Tours: hourly (on the hour) Mon–Sat. Admission charge

Loch Lomond & its islands

Loch Lomond is the largest body of fresh water in Britain. Roughly triangular, the loch is some 38 km (24 miles) from north to south and 6 km (4 miles) across at its widest, and reaches depths of 190 m (623 ft). From the loch, the River Leven flows southwest to meet the Clyde at Dumbarton. It's a lovely place to visit at any time of year, but undeniably at its most attractive in summer, when the still waters of the loch reflect the greenery of birch and beech woodland all around it. One of the finest (and most accessible) panoramic views is from the top of aptly named Conic Hill, at Balmaha on the east shore of the loch – it takes about 90 minutes to climb to the top, 358 m (1,164 ft) above sea level, from the Balmaha village car park. Wildife in the national park includes raptors such as the golden eagle and the osprey, winter migrant waterfowl including goldeneye ducks, whooper swans and white-fronted geese, and red and fallow deer. The loch is dotted with around 20 islands, each with its own picturesque history. Some are accessible if you have your own boat, others are privately owned and off limits to visitors. The largest, and most accessible, is Inchmurrin, where early medieval monks built a chapel dedicated to St Mirren ('inch' is the Gaelic word for 'island', hence 'Inchmuirren' means 'Mirren's Island'). Since the 1930s, the island has been farmed by the Scott family, who offer summer accommodation in self-catering chalets and cottages on the farm and operate a licensed bar and restaurant for day visitors.

◆ *Dumbarton Castle looks out over the Firth of Clyde*

Other islands on the loch include Clairinch and Inch Cailloch, both of which are managed by Scottish Natural Heritage and can be visited by arrangement. Inchmoan and Inchtavannach are managed by Luss Estates, one of the biggest local landowners. Inchfad and Inchcruin are privately owned and Inchconnachan is home to more than 40 wallabies, which were introduced to the island by Lady Arran in 1980. Two smaller islands are said to have connections with two great Scottish patriots. Inchlonaig ('island of yews') is said to have been planted with yew trees to provide wood to make bows for Robert the Bruce's army – a long-term project if ever there was one, as the slow-growing yew takes decades or centuries to mature. Wallace's Island is, of course, claimed to have been one of William Wallace's hideouts – but it's rather more likely that the island simply belonged to a landowner of the same name.

Loch Lomond & The Trossachs National Park ☎ 0845 345 4978 ⓦ www.lochlomond-trossachs.org. (Visitor centre has interactive exhibition, tourist information centre and guided tours by park rangers at Loch Lomond Shores, Balloch.)
Visitor centres at Luss ☎ 01301 702785 and **Balmaha** ☎ 01360 870470
Countryside Ranger Service ⓐ Balloch Public Slipway, Pier Road, Balloch ☎ 01389 757295

ACTIVITIES

Loch Lomond and its surroundings offer a huge choice of outdoor activities ranging from gentle lochside strolls to strenuous mountain hiking, long-distance walking and rock climbing. Dumbarton Rock offers one of the world's toughest technical climbs.

Adrenaline sports

The **Go Outdoors Initiative** (☎ 08707 200642
ⓦ www.gosmileoutdoors.co.uk) is a consortium of local businesses
offering 40 challenging outdoor activities, including abseiling,
power kiting, clay pigeon shooting, angling, pony trekking, climbing,
wakeboarding and windsurfing.

Cruises on Loch Lomond

Take a cruise on the loch aboard the elegant paddle steamer *Maid of
the Loch*. Launched in 1953 and restored and put back in operation
for its 50th anniversary, she sails several times daily in summer
from The Pier, Balloch (next to the Loch Lomond Shores outlet
centre). Other cruise operators with more modern vessels include:
Balloch: **Sweeney's Cruises** (☎ 01389 752376
ⓦ www.sweeney.uk.com) and **Mullens Cruises** (☎ 01389 751481)
Balmaha: **McFarlane and Son** ☎ 01360 870214
Tarbet: **Cruise Loch Lomond** ☎ 01301 702356

LUSS ONSCREEN

If Luss looks oddly familiar, that's because this designated
conservation village has been used as a location for a number
of film and TV productions – most recently the STV series
Take the High Road. Luss is far and away the prettiest of the
lochside villages, with neat little cottages laid out along
narrow streets. It was built by one of the less unpleasant local
lairds as a model village for his tenants in the 19th century,
and has a number of nice places to stay, several pleasant
pubs and restaurants, and a scattering of quite stylish gift and
craft shops.

Cycling

The Glasgow to Loch Lomond Cycleway (National Cycle Route Network 75) stretches 34 km (21 miles) from Glasgow city centre to Loch Lomond, then carries on all the way to Killin in Perthshire, following decommissioned railway tracks, canal towpaths, side roads and forest trails. For details contact **Sustrans** (☎ 0131 539 8122 ⓦ www.sustrans.org.uk) or visit ⓦ www.cyclingscotland.com

Sailing & boating

Loch Lomond is popular with yacht and dinghy sailors and powerboat sailors (who have objected strenuously to the national park's proposals to impose strict speed limits on the loch to protect wildlife). You can rent sailing boats and powerboats at several marinas at Balloch and nearby.

Walking

With 20 munros (summits over 914 m/3,000 ft), the Trossachs offer energetic hill walking on Glasgow's doorstep.

Additionally, Scotland's finest long-distance walking route, the West Highland Way, starts in Milngavie, on the northwest outskirts

WARNING FOR WALKERS

❶ Come prepared for changeable weather at any time of year. Good boots and waterproof outerwear are essential, even in summer, and proper planning and preparation are vital for winter walks on the hills, with snow and freezing temperatures possible from October until the end of May on higher ground.

of Glasgow, and passes through the national park on its way to Fort William, on the west coast. ❸ Douglas St, Milngavie ❶ 01389 722025 ⓦ www.west-highland-way.co.uk

RETAIL THERAPY

Auchentoshan Distillery Shop For whisky lovers this shop offers a full range of lowland single malt whiskies from the famous distillery (see page 120), as well as glassware, hip flasks and other dram-related paraphernalia. ❸ Dalmuir, Clydebank ❶ 01389 878561 ⓦ www.auchentoshan.com ❶ Guided tours: 10.00–16.00 Mon–Sat. Admission charge

⬥ Loch Lomond offers breathtaking scenery

Loch Lomond Shores This large outlet shopping mall and leisure centre sits slightly incongruously at the south end of Loch Lomond, on the outskirts of Balloch. Retailers include a number of Scotland's biggest names as well as international brands, a giant film screen shows the Legend of Loch Lomond presentation, and there is a children's play area. ⓐ Balloch ⓣ 01389 222406 ⓦ www.lochlomondshores.com ⓛ Usually 9.30–20.00 daily, but hours vary – consult website

TAKING A BREAK

Balloch
La Scarpetta £ ❶   Good, simple and inexpensive southern Italian cooking. ⓐ Balloch Road, Balloch ⓣ 01389 758247

Meson del Lago £ ❷   Restaurant, bar and tapas bar within the Lomond Shores complex, serving Mediterranean meals, snacks and cocktails. The outdoor terrace has great views up the loch. ⓐ Lomond Shores, Balloch ⓣ 01389 753834

Windows on the Loch ££ ❸   The restaurant of the Duck Bay Hotel is well named, with great views of the loch and Ben Lomond, a classic à la carte menu and a casual dining area. The wine list is extensive and features Old and New World wines. ⓐ Arden, by Balloch ⓣ 01389 751234

Luss
The Coach House £ ❹   Very popular tearoom and restaurant serving good snacks and meals all day. It gets very busy in summer and at weekends, when Luss is thronged with visitors. ⓣ 01436 860341

ACCOMMODATION

Accommodation in the region ranges from basic bed and breakfast to historic coaching inns and luxurious modern spa hotels. A wide range of places to stay to suit all budgets can be found and booked online at ⓦ www.visit-lochlomond.com

Rowardennan Hotel £ This cosy 3-star hotel's modern facilities – including two bars and a good restaurant – belie its 310-year history as a country inn. ⓐ Rowardennan village
ⓔ rowardennanhotel@visit-lochlomond.com

Black Bull Hotel ££ Very comfortable 19th-century coaching inn in Killearn in the foothills of the Trossachs with en-suite facilities, room service and a stylish, award-winning restaurant. ⓐ 2 The Square, Killearn ⓣ 01360 550215 ⓦ www.blackbullhotel.com

De Vere Cameron House Hotel ££ The 5-star Cameron House combines country-house ambience with modern luxuries such as an upmarket spa and beauty centre and a huge, heated indoor pool. A marina and yacht club are next door. ⓐ Arden, by Balloch
ⓣ 01389 755565 ⓦ www.devere.co.uk

The Lodge on Loch Lomond £££ The most luxurious hotel on the loch has hosted heads of state and offers a range of sybaritic rooms and suites along with its own spa and one of the best restaurants in the area, Colquhoun's. ⓐ Luss ⓣ 01436 860201
ⓔ res@loch-lomond.co.uk

Stirling & Stirlingshire

Scotland's fifth-largest city – after Glasgow, Edinburgh, Aberdeen and Dundee – is also its newest. Stirling was declared a city as recently as 2002, as part of the Queen's Golden Jubilee Celebrations. For all that, Stirling and the surrounding area are rich in history. The city's name means 'place of strife', and it's best known as the site of two rare Scottish victories in the 14th-century Wars of Independence. Stirling Bridge was where William Wallace's spearmen defeated the troops of King Edward I of England (who was nicknamed 'Langshanks' by the Scots) and Bannockburn, where Robert the Bruce's foot-soldiers gave the very best of Edward II's knights another sound beating and, as it says in Scotland's unofficial national anthem 'Flower of Scotland', 'sent them homeward to think again'. Arriving in Stirling, it's easy to see why it has such a pivotal role in Scottish history – its forbidding castle, atop a high crag, commanded the most important route between southern and northern Scotland, and without holding Stirling no invader could hope to conquer the country. The castle is Stirling's most prominent landmark, with the narrow streets of the Old Town stretching eastwards from its gateway towards the banks of the Forth.

GETTING THERE

The easiest way to get to Stirling is by train from Glasgow Queen Street Station (35 minutes; Scotrail ☎ 08457 550033 ⊛ www.scotrail.co.uk).

Alternatively, buses leave from Buchanan Bus Station in Glasgow city centre, operated by First (☎ 0141 423 6600 ⊛ www.firstgroup.com) and Scottish Citylink Coaches (☎ 08705 50 50 50).

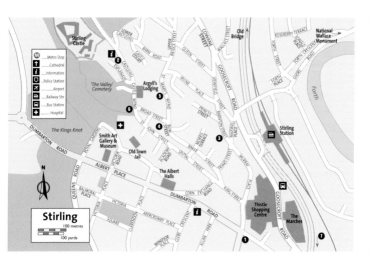

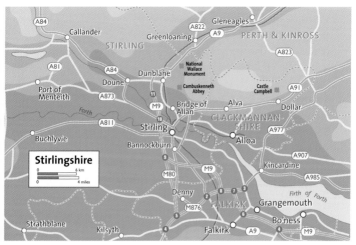

TOURIST BOARDS
Trossachs Tourist Board ⓐ 7 Alexandra Parade, Dunoon
ⓣ 08707 200 629 ⓦ www.visitscottishheartlands.com
Stirling Tourist Information Centre ⓐ 41 Dumbarton Road
ⓣ 01786 479901 ⓔ info@stirling.visitscotland.com

SIGHTS & ATTRACTIONS

Bannockburn & Bannockburn Heritage Centre

South of Stirling, outside the Bannockburn Heritage Centre, a statue of Robert the Bruce mounted on his charger gazes over the site of his famous 1314 victory over Edward II. Inside there are plans of the battlefield, life-size representations of Bruce, Wallace and other warriors of the day, shields and battle banners. In summer, there are frequent Living History presentations and storytelling sessions, and kids can dress up in period costume and try on armour and chain-mail. ⓐ Glasgow Road 4 km (2 miles) south of Stirling off M80 motorway ⓣ 01786 812664 ⓦ www.nts.org.uk ⓛ 10.30–16.00 Mar & Nov; 10.00–17.30 Apr–Oct. Admission charge

Callander & Rob Roy & Trossachs Visitor Centre

The small market town of Callander lies 26 km (16 miles) north of Stirling on the A84 and is surrounded by rolling farmland, with the Trossach hills as a backdrop. It's worth a visit just for the colourful Rob Roy and Trossachs Visitor Centre, which celebrates the famous outlaw's life and contrasts the romantic legend created by Sir Walter Scott in the 19th century (and perpetuated by actor Liam Neeson in the eponymous 1995 film) with the rather grimmer and grittier reality of Rob Roy McGregor's life and times.

ⓐ Ancaster Square, Callander ☎ 01877 330342 🕐 11.00–15.00 Mon–Fri, 11.00–16.00 Sat & Sun, Jan & Feb; 10.00–17.00 Mar–May & Oct–Dec; 9.30–18.00 June & Sept; 9.00–18.00 July & Aug

Cambuskenneth Abbey

Founded by the Augustinian order in 1147, the abbey lies in picturesque ruins just outside Stirling. Though only its tower still stands, this was once a grand and influential religious foundation, where Robert the Bruce convened Scotland's first parliament after his victories over England in 1326.

ⓐ 2 km (1 mile) east of Stirling town centre ☎ 0131 668 8800 ⓦ www.historic-scotland.gov.uk 🕐 24 hrs (no access to interior)

Castle Campbell

This dour stronghold was one of the eastern outposts of the Campbell clan, whose lands stretched from Argyll on the west coast as far east as Perthshire. Poised between the Highlands and Lowlands, the Campbell potentates used their strategic position to their advantage and became the most powerful of the clan names, with a canny ability to pick the winning side in Scotland's centuries of strife. Their aristocratic descendants are still among the wealthiest and greatest landowners in Scotland. Built in the 15th century, the partly ruined castle is surrounded by terraced gardens and looks out over the picturesque woodlands of Dollar Glen. You can get there by car, or by bus from Stirling – in summer, it's a very pleasant and quite energetic 20-minute walk from the Dollar Glen bus stop through the wooded glen.

ⓐ 16 km (10 miles) east of Stirling on the A91 ☎ 01259 742408 ⓦ www.historic-scotland.gov.uk 🕐 9.30–18.30 Apr–Sept; 9.30–16.30 Mon–Thur, 14.00–16.30 Sun, Oct–Mar. Admission charge

Doune & Doune Castle

Doune, 13 km (8 miles) northwest of Stirling, was traditionally a meeting place between the wild clanspeople of the Scottish Highlands and the more civilised folk of the Lowlands. Highlanders brought cattle to sell and bought Lowland products such as textiles and firearms including the famous Doune flintlock pistols. Doune is a pretty little village, and the splendid 14th-century Doune Castle with its grand hall was a seat of the Stewart Earls of Moray.

Castle Road ● 01786 841742 ● www.historic-scotland.gov.uk
● 9.30–18.00 Apr–Sept; 9.30–17.00 Oct–Mar. Admission charge

Dunblane, Dunblane Cathedral & Dunblane Museum

Dunblane, standing in the glen of the Allan Water 10 km (6 miles) north of Stirling, has one imposing landmark – its gracious cathedral, founded during the reign of King David I and lavishly restored in 1892, with vivid stained-glass windows that were added in the early 20th century. Dunblane Museum, housed in the vaults of a 17th-century mansion, has a collection that highlights the history of the next-door cathedral and the life of its founder, the eponymous St Blane.

The Cross ● 01765 823440 ● www.dunblanemuseum.org.uk
● 10.30–16.30 Mon–Sat, May–Sept

DUNBLANE TOURIST INFORMATION CENTRE

Dunblane Tourist Information Centre ● Stirling Road
● 08707 200 613 ● info@dunblane.visitscotland.com
● May–Sept

Falkirk, Callendar House & the Falkirk Wheel

Falkirk, 19 km (12 miles) south of Stirling, is now almost entirely a residential suburb, poised midway between Glasgow and Edinburgh. That said, it has a handful of attractions spanning 2,000 years of history, from the Roman Empire to the heyday of the Industrial Revolution. Callendar House is a stately home that, in its day, hosted Mary Queen of Scots, Oliver Cromwell and Bonnie Prince Charlie among other notables. Its varied exhibits are an interesting introduction to the region's history, especially the Industrial Revolution of the 18th and 19th centuries, when Falkirk was transformed from a small market town into a major powerhouse of the Age of Steam.

But the town's biggest attraction is the Falkirk Wheel. Completed in 2002, this stunning piece of 21st-century engineering is visually remarkable in its own right and has reconnected two equally remarkable feats of 18th-century engineering – the Forth and Clyde Canal and the Union Canal, one 35 m (115 ft) above the other. This huge boat-lift now hoists boats between the two waterways, which have been reborn as a superb leisure resource for Scotland. It's amazing just to watch the Wheel in action from the Visitor Centre, and you can also board a boat to ride the Wheel and the two canals.

In AD 82 the Roman general Agricola brought his legions into Caledonia and defeated the massed Pictish tribes at the Battle of Mons Graupius – a famous victory. But after this triumph the Romans promptly fell back, and in AD 122 Emperor Hadrian subsequently ordered the building of a coast-to-coast rampart to keep the Picts at bay. His more ambitious successor, Antoninus Pius, pushed north again and built a new defensive line, the Antonine Wall, between the Forth and Clyde estuaries. This 60-km (37-mile) fortification was abandoned less than 20 years later, but remnants of it can be seen near Falkirk.

Antonine Wall ⓐ next to the A803 east of Bonnybridge, 19 km
(12 miles) south of Stirling ⓣ 0131 668 8800
ⓦ www.historic-scotland.gov.uk
Callendar House ⓐ Callendar Park, Falkirk ⓣ 01324 503770
ⓦ www.falkirk.gov.uk ⓛ 10.00–17.00 Mon–Sat. Admission charge
Falkirk Wheel ⓐ Lime Road, Tamfourhill, Falkirk ⓣ 08700 500 208
ⓦ www.thefalkirkwheel.co.uk ⓛ 9.00–18.30 Apr–Oct, 10.00–17.00
Nov–Mar
Tourist Information Centre ⓐ 2/4 Glebe Street ⓣ 08707 200 614
ⓔ info@falkirk.visitscotland.com

National Wallace Monument

On the outskirts of Stirling, and just as prominent a landmark as
the castle itself, is the Wallace Monument, standing on a hilltop
above the surrounding farmlands. The monument looms above
a recent statue of Wallace. Jarringly, his features are those not
of a medieval Scottish warlord but of an Australian–American
film star, Mel Gibson, who played Wallace in the movie *Braveheart*
in 1995.

ⓐ Abbey Craig, Hillfoot Road, Stirling, 3 km (1.5 miles) north of the
town centre ⓛ 10.30–16.00 Jan, Feb, Nov & Dec; 10.00–17.00
Mar–May & Oct; 10.00–18.00 June; 9.30–18.30 July & Aug;
9.30–17.30 Sept. Admission charge

Stirling

Argyll's Lodging Facing the castle gateway, this lodging was built in
the 17th century as the home of Sir William Alexander, who later
became Earl of Stirling, and is the most complete and impressive
example of an aristocratic townhouse of that era.

Smith Art Gallery & Museum This gallery is well worth a visit for its eclectic collection of objects from around the world – most of them donated by local people who had lived and worked abroad as engineers, soldiers, doctors and administrators during the heyday of the British Empire. The museum was a bequest to the city by painter and collector Thomas Stuart Smith (1815–69) and its art gallery

▲ *The Victorian Gothic monument to William Wallace*

displays a plethora of landscapes, battlefield scenes and portraits of local bigwigs, the high point of which (if a plethora can have a high point) is the portrait of the Young Pretender, Charles Edward Stuart – better known as Bonnie Prince Charlie.

ⓐ Dumbarton Road ⓣ 01786 471917 ⓦ www.smithartgallery.demon.co.uk ⓛ 10.30–17.00 Tues–Sat, 14.00–17.00 Sun

Stirling Castle Not for nothing is Stirling Castle known as 'the key to the kingdom'. From its ramparts, 76 m (250 ft) above sea level, there are sweeping views of the lowlands below and the River Forth,

◑ The forbidding exterior of Stirling Castle

though the battlefield of Bannockburn is now covered with suburban homes. The castle's grim exterior belies a more genteel world within, with landscaped gardens and a splendid royal palace. Its Great Hall, which was built during the reign of King James IV and embellished by Renaissance wings built for his successor, James V, is the largest hall of any Scottish palace or castle, and the palace is a masterpiece of Renaissance design. Mary, Queen of Scots was crowned in the castle's Royal Chapel in 1543 and her son James was baptised there in 1534. After the Union of the Crowns of Scotland and England in 1603 – when James VI of Scotland also became James I of England – Stirling lost its key role as a royal residence, but the castle remained strategically important in the troubled times of the late 17th and early 18th centuries. The castle houses the regimental museum of the Argyll and Sutherland Highlanders, the oldest of Britain's kilted Highland regiments. History aside, the castle is now also an occasional venue for open-air performances by classical music ensembles and rock bands on summer evenings.
ⓐ Castle Wynd ⓣ 01786 450000 ⓦ www.historic-scotland.gov.uk
ⓛ 9.30–18.00 Apr–Sept; 9.30–17.00, Oct–Mar. Admission charge includes Argyll's Lodging (same opening hours).

Stirling Old Bridge This stands roughly where Wallace's Scottish freedom fighters won their first victory against Edward I. Built in the late 15th century – almost two centuries after that fight – it was blown up in 1745 to delay the advance of Bonnie Prince Charlie's Highlanders, and repaired four years later.
ⓐ Off the A9 ⓣ 0131 668 8800 ⓦ www.historic-scotland.gov.uk

Stirling Old Town Jail Across Castle Wynd from Argyll's Lodging is a Victorian prison that has been turned into a slightly kitsch visitor

attraction with actors playing out the roles of convicts, warders and hangmen.

🚇 St John Street 📞 01786 450050 🕐 9.30–17.30 Apr–Sept; 9.30–16.30 Mar–Oct. Admission charge

ACTIVITIES

Blair Drummond Safari & Adventure Park

Wallabies, chimps, elephants and camels are among the exotic beasts that can be enjoyed here. There's also a theme park with water rides and bumper cars among other attractions.

🚇 Between Doune and Stirling on the A84 📞 01786 841456 🌐 www.blairdrummond.com 🕐 10.00–19.30 Mar–Oct

Falkirk Wheel Boat Trips

Board a modern canal cruiser for a dizzying 35-m (115-ft) ride on the Falkirk Wheel, then cruise through the Union Canal's Roughcastle Tunnel before descending again to the Forth and Clyde Canal.

🚇 Falkirk Wheel, Lime Road, Tamfourhill, Falkirk 📞 08700 500 208 🌐 www.thefalkirkwheel.co.uk 🕐 Boat trips: 11.00–15.10 hourly. Admission charge; booking necessary

Ochil Hills

Within sight of Stirling, the rolling Ochil Hills are perfect for undemanding weekend walking. The summit of Ben Cleuch, the highest of this range of gentle hills, is just 721 m (2600 ft) above sea level, and on a clear summer day it affords fabulous views of the Firth of Forth, all the way down to the bridges.

For escorted walks contact C-N-Do 🚇 32 Stirling Enterprise Park 📞 01786 445703 🌐 www.cndoscotland.com

Stirling Ghost Walk

A spooky, guided walk through the haunted, cobbled wynds (alleyways) of the Old Town, below the castle.

Bookings and information from Stirling Tourist Information Centre ☎ 01592 872788.

TAKING A BREAK

Peckham's £ ❶ This combination delicatessen and bistro – part of a chain with outlets in Glasgow and Edinburgh – is affordable luxury, with imaginative, Mediterranean-influenced cooking and a well-priced wine list. ⓐ 52 Port Street, Stirling ☎ 01786 447047

Portcullis £ ❷ This cosy pub-restaurant is in a converted 18th-century schoolhouse a stone's throw from Stirling Castle and serves substantial pub meals as well as a choice of ales and wines. ⓐ Castle Wynd, Stirling ☎ 01786 472290

Smiling Jack's £ ❸ Extremely cheap – considering the size of the portions – and very cheerful, this Tex-Mex joint is for those with a hearty appetite to satisfy. ⓐ 17 Barnton Street, Stirling ☎ 01786 462809

The Tollbooth £ ❹ Bright, modern café-bar within Stirling's lively arts centre, handy for the castle and Old Town sights. ⓐ Jail Wynd, Stirling ☎ 01786 274010

Whistlebinkies £ ❺ A great place for a lunchtime pie and a pint, and smokers will appreciate the outdoor beer garden. Live music in the evening. ⓐ 73/75 St Mary's Wynd, Stirling ☎ 01786 451256

Herman's ££ ❻ Launched in 2004, Herman's is simply the best restaurant in Stirling, serving simple, fresh Scottish seafood, game and local produce, elegantly prepared. ⓐ Mar Place House, Stirling ① 01786 450632

Jekyll's ££ ❼ Stylish hotel restaurant – the only place in town that can compete with Herman's, and surprisingly good value despite its upmarket pretensions. ⓐ Queen's Hotel, 24 Henderson Street, Stirling ① 01786 833268

ACCOMMODATION

Glenardoch House £ A charming B&B set in an 18th-century house on the banks of the river and in the shadow of Doune Castle, with extensive gardens. ⓐ Castle Road, Doune ① 0845 22 55 121 ⓦ www.glenardochhouse.com

Park Lodge Country House Hotel £ Excellent value in this Georgian hotel with views of the castle. ⓐ 32 Park Terrace, Stirling ① 0845 22 55 121

Stirling Highland Hotel ££ A former Victorian school in the centre of Stirling now makes for a wonderfully elegant place to stay in the city. There's also a leisure club on site. ⓐ Spittal Street, Stirling ① 08701 160602 ⓦ www.paramount-hotels.co.uk

---

▶ *Kelvingrove Park is a great place to relax and have fun*

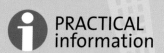

PRACTICAL
information

Directory

GETTING THERE

By air

Glasgow International Airport is serviced by several daily scheduled flights from major British and European cities, and there are some 40 flights a day from London to Glasgow operated by British Airways and other airlines. Flight time from London is 1 hour. International flights cover Asian, African, Australian and US destinations, as well as all over Europe. Scotland's own no-frills airline, Flyglobespan, also has many flights between Glasgow and Europe. The low-cost no-frills airline Ryanair (ⓦ www.ryanair.com) operates flights from the rest of Britain and Europe from Glasgow Prestwick International Airport.

Many people are aware that air travel emits CO_2, which contributes to climate change. You may be interested in the possibility of lessening the environmental impact of your flight through the charity Climate Care, which offsets your CO_2 by funding environmental projects around the world. Visit www.climatecare.org

By rail

The GNER rail route from London King's Cross to Glasgow Central Station is a journey time of approximately 5½ hours on the direct route, although some services require a change of trains at Edinburgh. **GNER:** ⓞ 08457 48 49 50 ⓦ www.gner.co.uk

By coach

National Express coaches make the journey between London and Glasgow seven times a day, with an average journey time of between 8½ and 10 hours, depending on traffic and time of day. Megabus is a budget coach service that also links Glasgow with London and runs three services a day, one of which is overnight.

Megabus ☎ 0901 331 0031 🌐 www.megabus.com
National Express ☎ 08705 808080 🌐 www.nationalexpress.com

Driving

Glasgow is easily reached by the M6/M74 motorway from the west of Britain and by the M8 from Edinburgh. Both the AA and the RAC offer route-planning services on their websites to help plan your journey.

AA 🌐 www.theaa.com
RAC 🌐 www.rac.co.uk

ENTRY FORMALITIES
Documentation

Valid passports are the only documentation required for entry into Great Britain for visitors from the Republic of Ireland, USA, Canada, Australia, New Zealand, South Africa and members of the EU for a stay of up to six months. Other visitors should consult the British Embassy in their own country about visa requirements or check 🌐 www.ukvisas.gov.uk

Customs

There are almost no restrictions on what legal goods can be imported or exported to and from other EU countries, as long as you can prove that they are for your own use and not for resale. Anything more than 3,000 cigarettes or 90 litres of wine, for instance, would be considered suspicious and questions will be asked. To import tobacco or alcohol you must be over 17 years of age.

For visitors from outside the EU, the restrictions on importing are as follows:

- 200 cigarettes; or 100 cigarillos; or 50 cigars; or 250 g of tobacco
- 60 cc of perfume
- 2 litres of still table wine
- 250 cc of eau de toilette
- 1 litre of spirits or strong liqueurs over 22 per cent volume; or 2 litres of fortified wine, sparkling wine or other liqueurs
- £145 worth of all other goods including gifts and souvenirs.

MONEY

The pound (£) is the official currency of Great Britain. £1 = 100 pence. It comes in notes of £5, £10, £20, £50 and £100. Coins are in denominations of £1 and £2, and 1, 2, 5, 10, 20 and 50 pence. One aspect that often confuses visitors to Scotland is that Scottish banknotes come in three different designs, representing the Bank of Scotland, the Royal Bank of Scotland and the Clydesdale Bank. English banknotes are, however, entirely legal tender in Scotland.

ATM machines (known as cashpoints) can be found outside banks and many other areas, and are open 24 hours a day. The most widely accepted credit cards are VISA and Mastercard, but American Express is also accepted in larger hotels and more expensive

SCOTTISH BANK NOTES

🛈 It might be advisable to change Scottish banknotes back into English banknotes at the end of your stay. Even in England, where they are also legal tender, many smaller shopkeepers can be confused by them and refuse to take them, and they are extremely difficult to exchange abroad.

restaurants and shops. Traveller's cheques and foreign money can be exchanged at larger banks and at bureaux de change.

HEALTH, SAFETY AND CRIME

Visitors to Scotland are unlikely to encounter any food or drink issues – tap water is safe to drink, although bottled water is also available everywhere.

Medical facilities are run by the National Health Service (NHS), which entitles British and EU citizens to free medical care. Visitors from outside these areas should make sure they have adequate health insurance to avoid having to pay for any medical care should they fall ill. If you take prescriptive drugs, make sure you bring an adequate supply as well as a letter from your doctor or personal health record card. Most minor ailments can be diagnosed and

▲ *Stirling Old Bridge is one of Scotland's most historic locations*

treated at pharmacies throughout the city and, unlike many other countries, mild pain relief, such as aspirin, can often be bought at small grocery shops and in supermarkets, as well as at pharmacies.

Glasgow is generally a safe city, particularly in the tourist areas, but common sense applies as it does everywhere in terms of personal possessions. In crowded areas and in pubs keep an eye on bags and wallets. Large crowds of Celtic and Rangers football supporters are probably best avoided on match days. Any crime should be reported to the police straightaway. Police can be seen regularly on the streets, dressed in black and white uniform and, often, fluorescent yellow jackets. They are friendly and efficient, and can be approached for anything from asking directions to reporting crime.

For advice on what to do in an emergency, see page 186.

LOST PROPERTY

If you lose any of your belongings through negligence rather than theft, you can contact any police station or the city's main lost property office (0141 221 8597). If you leave any belongings on a train, contact First ScotRail (0141 335 3276).

OPENING HOURS

Shops: 09.00–17.30 Mon–Sat. Some shops and department stores also open later until 19.00 or 20.00 on Wednesdays or Thursdays, and have shorter opening hours on Sundays.

Banks: 09.30–16.30 Mon–Fri. Some banks are also open on Saturday mornings. Cash can be obtained 24 hours a day from hole-in-the-wall ATMs.

Attractions: opening hours for individual attractions are given next to their listing in the book.

TOILETS

Toilet facilities can be found in museums, department stores and shopping centres, and are generally clean and of a high standard. In pubs you would normally be expected to buy a drink before using the facilities, although many landlords and bar staff will kindly overlook this.

CHILDREN

Glasgow is a child-friendly city and with the smoking ban in place even most pubs will be happy to have children on their premises, although it's always best to check first. All but the top restaurants will welcome children, and many offer children's menus. Breast-feeding in pubs and restaurants, however, is generally considered taboo.

Many attractions are specifically geared towards children, including the Glasgow Science Centre (see page 94), the Scotland Street School Museum (see page 100), and the Scottish Mask and Puppet Centre (ⓐ 8–10 Balcarres Avenue ⓣ 0141 339 6185), where they can learn to make puppets and masks. Slightly older children will also get a lot out of the natural history section of the Kelvingrove Museum (see page 85). Just outside Glasgow in Tollcross Park there's also a Children's Zoo (ⓣ 0141 552 1142).

Baby food, nappies and other kiddie paraphernalia can be bought in supermarkets, in high-street chains such as Boots the Chemists and at grocery stores.

COMMUNICATIONS

Phone

The phone numbers given in this book are local numbers including the Glasgow area code of ☎ 0141.

Public payphones accept coins, phonecards or credit cards. Phonecards are available from post offices and newsagents in different values from £2.00 to £20.00. Some payphones also offer the option of texting messages. The minimum rate for a cash call is 30 pence; the minimum rate for a credit card call is 95 pence. As in the rest of the world, making phone calls from hotel rooms is exorbitantly expensive, so best avoided if possible.

Post

The British postal service is generally very reliable, with first-class mail arriving at UK destinations usually within one day, and in

---

TELEPHONING TO AND FROM GLASGOW

Telephoning Glasgow from abroad: dial 00 44 141 followed by the local number.

Telephoning abroad:

Australia 00 61
Canada 00 1
Republic of Ireland 00 353
New Zealand 00 64
South Africa 00 27
USA 00 1

National Operator Service 100
International Operator Service 155
Directory Enquiries 118 118

Europe within two or three days (depending on the service at the country of destination). The main post office in the city centre is in St Vincent Street, but there are other central branches in Merchant City and on Bothwell Street and Hope Street. Post offices are usually open all day (09.00–17.30 Mon–Fri and 09.00–noon Sat), although smaller branches often close for lunch. Stamps can be bought at post offices, as well as at larger newsagents. Post boxes on the street are the round, red pillar boxes, some of which have separate slots for national and international mail. For enquiries contact the Post Office Customer Helpline (☎ 0845 722 3344 ⓦ www.postoffice.co.uk).

Current rates for sending postcards are:
United Kingdom 32p (first class) or 23p (second class)
Europe 44p
Outside Europe 50p

Internet

The easyInternetcafé, established by the easyJet conglomerate, can be found at Kilmarnock Road, St Vincent Street and the Trongate Shopping Centre. All three are open seven days a week and offer great value at around £1.00 for an hour's worth of broadband access. Various other Internet cafés, however, are dotted all over the city and you're never likely to be more than a few minutes away from web and email access.

ELECTRICITY

The standard electrical voltage in Britain is 240 v with three square-pinned plugs. Foreign appliances will require an adaptor plug, available in your home country, and some US appliances running on 110 v may require a transformer.

TRAVELLERS WITH DISABILITIES

Many of Glasgow's older buildings, including pubs, may be difficult to access for wheelchair users – even if you are able to enter the establishment, you may not be able to use the toilet facilities. Newer establishments, however, including museums, restaurants and bars build disabled access into their design by law.

In general, Glasgow takes the issue of disability very seriously indeed.

Capability Scotland provides advice and information about disability issues, while the Glasgow Access Panel has an excellent website detailing disabled accessibility to all manner of places in the city, including churches, restaurants and shops. Holiday Care is a national organisation that offers advice about holidays around Britain and transport issues for those with disabilities. RADAR offers the same service, as well as advice for other countries.

Capability Scotland ⓐ 11 Ellersly Road, Edinburgh EH12 6HY ⓣ 0131 313 5510 ⓦ www.capability-scotland.org.uk
Glasgow Access Panel ⓐ 11 Queens Crescent, Glasgow ⓣ 0141 332 2444 ⓦ www.glasgowaccesspanel.org.uk
Holiday Care ⓐ 7th Floor, Sunley House, 4 Bedford Park, Croydon CR0 2AP ⓣ 0845 124 9971 (UK), 00 44 208 760 0072 (outside UK) ⓦ www.holidaycare.org.uk
RADAR ⓐ 12 City Forum, 250 City Road, London EC1V 8AF ⓣ 020 7250 3222 ⓦ www.radar.org.uk

TOURIST OFFICES

The city's main tourist office is centrally located at George Square near the bus station and stocks a range of leaflets, literature, guides and maps of the city and the surrounding area, as well as a small selection of souvenirs. Staff are knowledgeable and helpful, and can offer advice on attractions, eating out, current events, accommodation and theatre tickets (including handling bookings), day trips and much more. There's also a very good information centre at Glasgow International Airport, near the arrivals and departures area.

Glasgow and Clyde Valley Tourist Board ⓐ 11 George Square ⓣ 0141 566 0800 ⓦ www.seeglasgow.com ⓒ 09.00–18.00 Mon–Sat,

⬥ *The large shopping and leisure centre of Loch Lomond Shores*

10.00–18.00 Sun, Apr & Oct; 09.00–19.00 Mon–Sat, 10.00–19.00 Sun, May, June & Sept; 09. 00–20.00 Mon–Sat, 10.00–20.00 Sun, July–Aug; 09.00–17.00 Mon–Wed, 09.00–17.00 Thur–Sat, 10.00–17.00 Sun, Nov–Mar

Airport Information/Tourist Information Desk, Glasgow International Airport ☎ 0141 848 4400

Websites

The following websites also offer useful information:
www.glasgowguide.co.uk
www.historic-scotland.gov.uk
www.visitscotland.com
www.visitbritain.com

FURTHER READING
Non-fiction

Along Great Western Road: An Illustrated History of Glasgow's West End by Gordon R Urquhart (Stenlake Publishing, 2000).

Charles Rennie Mackintosh by John McKean (Colin Baxter Photography, 2005). A history of the man and his work, illustrated with examples.

Night Song of the Last Tram: A Glasgow Childhood by Robert Douglas (Hodder & Stoughton, 2005). Autobiographical account of growing up in a Glasgow tenement.

Once Upon a Time in Glasgow by John Watson (Neil Wilson Publishing Ltd, 2003). A full history of the city.

The Glasgow Almanac: An A–Z of the City and its People by Stephen Terry (Neil Wilson Publishing Ltd, 2005).

Weegies v Edinbuggers by Ian Black (Black and White, 2003). A humorous look at the rivalry between the two Scottish cities.

Fiction

Dick Donovan: The Glasgow Detective by James Emmerson Preston Muddock (Mercat Press, 2005). A reprint of the popular Victorian detective series.

Glasgow Tales by Rachel Hazelwood (ed.) (Endpapers, 2005). A collection of short stories set in the modern city.

How Late it Was, How Late by James Kelman (Vintage, 2004). The 1994 Booker Prize winner is a stream of consciousness tale about alcoholism and police brutality in rain-soaked Glasgow.

Lanark by Alasdair Gray (Canongate Classics, 2001). A blend of surrealism and realism set in the outskirts of Glasgow.

Para Handy by Neil Munro (Birlinn, 2002). A collection of Munro's classic tales of Clyde mariner Para Handy and his crew as they sail between Glasgow and the Highlands.

Rob Roy by Sir Walter Scott (Wordsworth Classics). The classic, heavily romanticised tale of Rob Roy McGregor.

The Trick is to Keep Breathing by Janice Galloway (Minerva, 1991). Acclaimed tale of living on a Glasgow housing scheme.

Emergencies

EMERGENCY NUMBERS

Police 999
Ambulance 999
Fire Brigade 999
Late-night Pharmacy The main late-night pharmacy is Munro Pharmacy ⓐ 693 Great Western Road ❶ 0141 339 0012 🕔 09.00–21.00. You can find other late-night pharmacies by looking at the list on the door of any closed pharmacy.

> **POLICE**
> The police headquarters for central Glasgow are
> ⓐ 50 Stewart Street ❶ 0141 532 3000
> The most central police station in Glasgow, however, is
> ⓐ 945 Argyle Street ❶ 0141 532 3200

MEDICAL EMERGENCIES

Hospitals

There are four main hospitals in Glasgow with accident and emergency departments:

Glasgow Royal Infirmary ⓐ Castle Street ❶ 0141 211 4000
Glasgow Western Infirmary ⓐ Dumbarton Road ❶ 0141 211 2000
Southern General Hospital ⓐ 1345 Govan Road ❶ 0141 201 1100
Stobhill Hospital ⓐ 133 Balornock Road ❶ 0141 201 3000

Dental

For dental problems visit the **Glasgow Dental Hospital**
ⓐ 378 Sauchiehall Street ❶ 0141 211 9600 🕔 09.00–15.00 Mon–Fri

CONSULATES AND EMBASSIES

There are no embassies or consulates for the following countries in Glasgow itself. The nearest branches are in Edinburgh as follows:

Australia @ Melrose House, 69 George Street ☎ 0131 624 3333

Canada @ 50 Lothian Road, Festival Square ☎ 0131 473 6320

New Zealand @ 5 Rutland Square ☎ 0131 222 8109

Republic of Ireland @ 16 Randolph Crescent ☎ 0131 226 7711

USA @ 3 Regent Terrace ☎ 0131 556 8315

● *Glasgow's cathedral dates from the 12th century*

The publishers would like to thank the following for supplying the copyright photographs for this book: p19 BBC Scottish Symphony Orchestra; p32 Epic Scotland; pp21, 127 Pictures Colour Library; p12 The Stand; all the rest Robin Gauldie.

Copy editor: Sandra Stafford
Proofreader: Emma Sangster

Send your thoughts to
books@thomascook.com

- Found a great bar, club, shop or must-see sight that we don't feature?

- Like to tip us off about any information that needs updating?

- Want to tell us what you love about this handy little guidebook and more importantly how we can make it even handier?

Then here's your chance to tell all! Send us ideas, discoveries and recommendations today and then look out for your valuable input in the next edition of this title. As an extra 'thank you' from Thomas Cook Publishing, you'll be automatically entered into our exciting monthly prize draw.

Send an email to the above address (stating the book's title) or write to: CitySpots Project Editor, Thomas Cook Publishing, PO Box 227, The Thomas Cook Business Park, Unit 18, Coningsby Road, Peterborough PE3 8SB, UK.